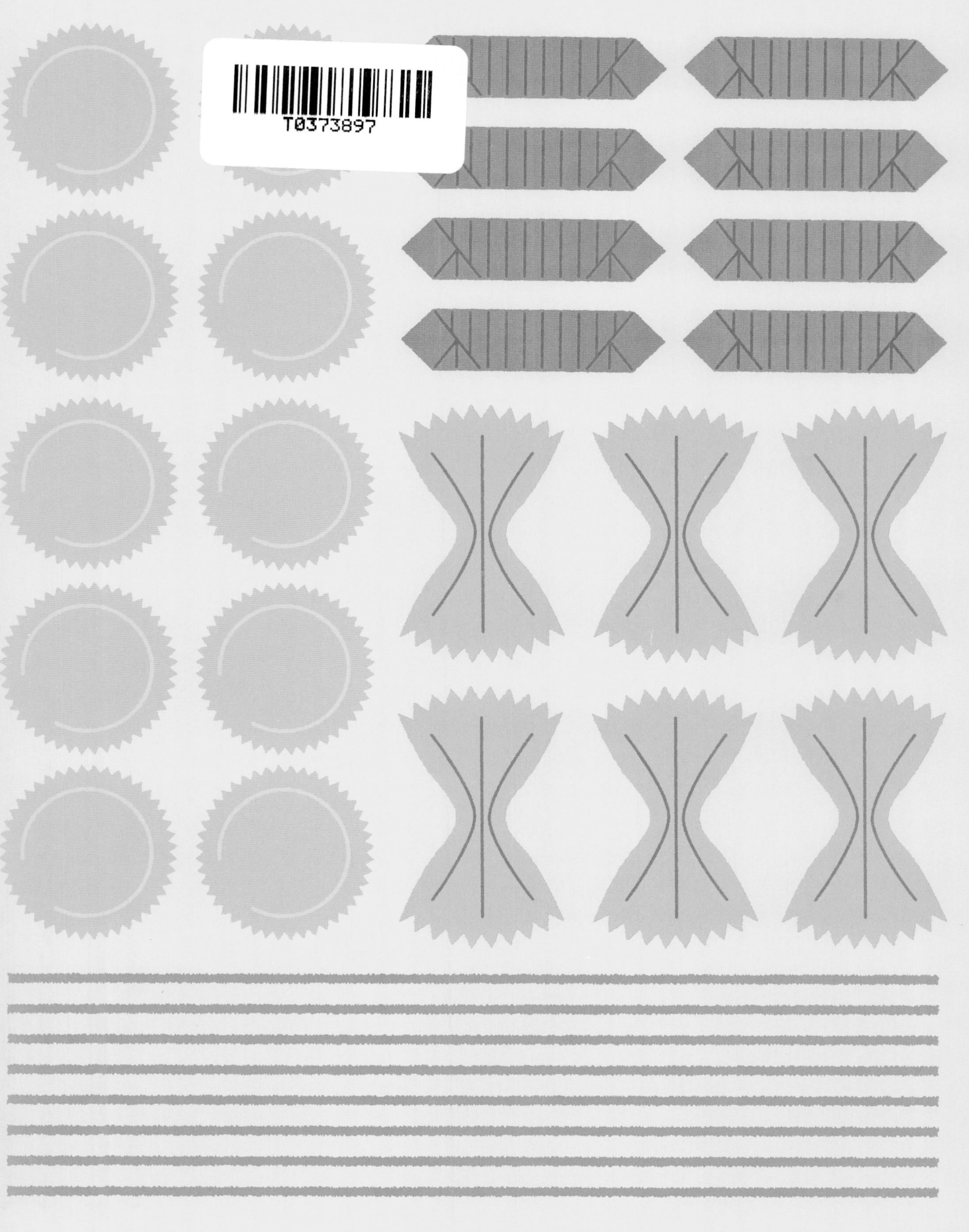

Pasta is a universal constant that keeps us grounded, not only in our past but also our present. In this book, Alec shares his journey of pasta through not only his eyes, but by creating new memories with his sons. As Alec says himself, 'Pasta is something so simple that it can be taught easily, repeated often and passed across language and culture barriers for generations.' *Pasta et Al* is a fun and curious adventure exploring the world of pasta!

JOE SASTO, CHEF AND PASTA EXPERT

A big-hearted, thoughtful cookbook that will teach you not only how to make beautiful, traditional pasta shapes but how to get playful and creative with colours and flavours too.

EMIKO DAVIES, AUTHOR OF *TORTELLINI AT MIDNIGHT*

Pasta et AI

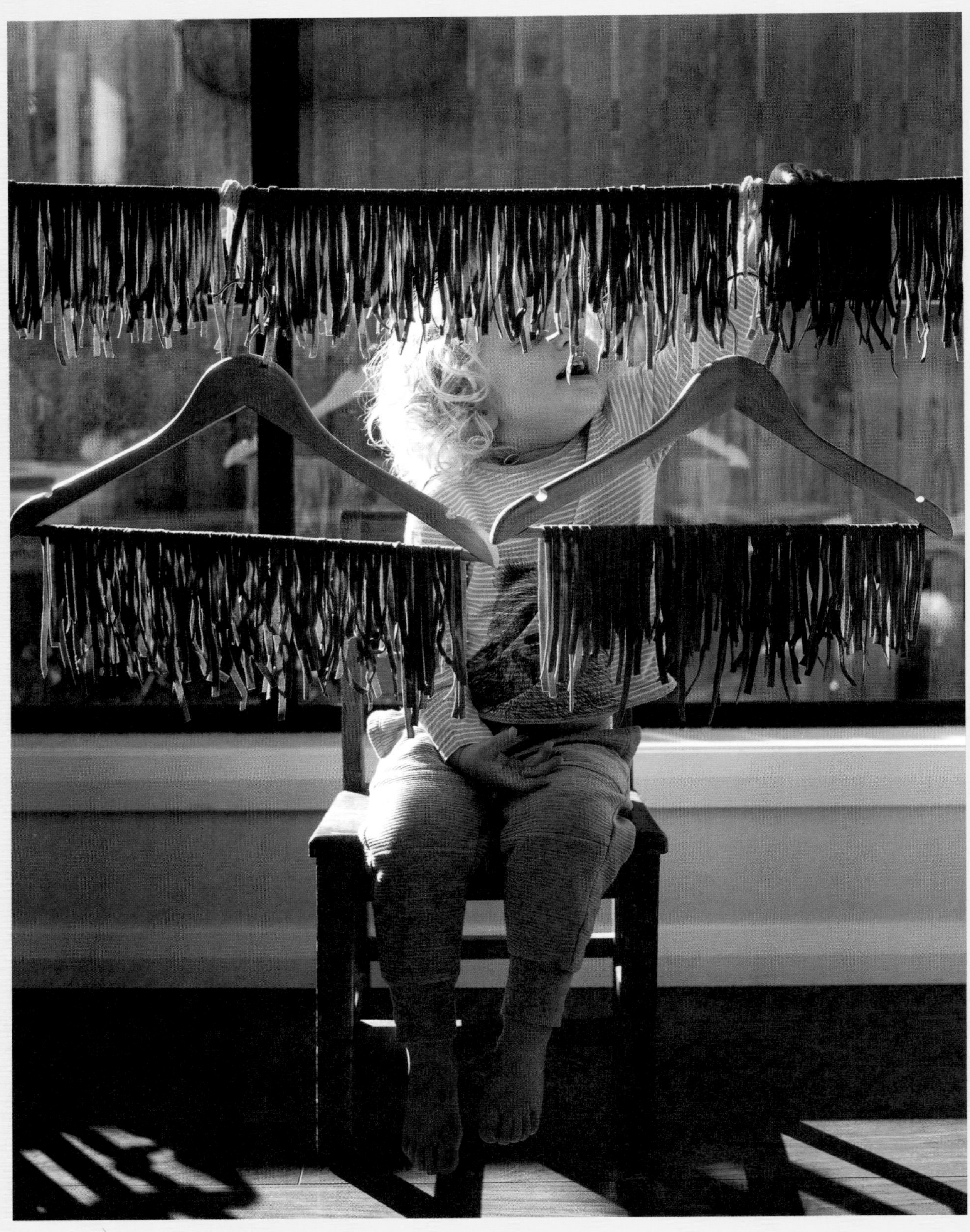

For Aldo and Elio

Pasta et Al

ALEC MORRIS

The Many Shapes of a Family Tradition

Hardie Grant

BOOKS

DOUGH 13

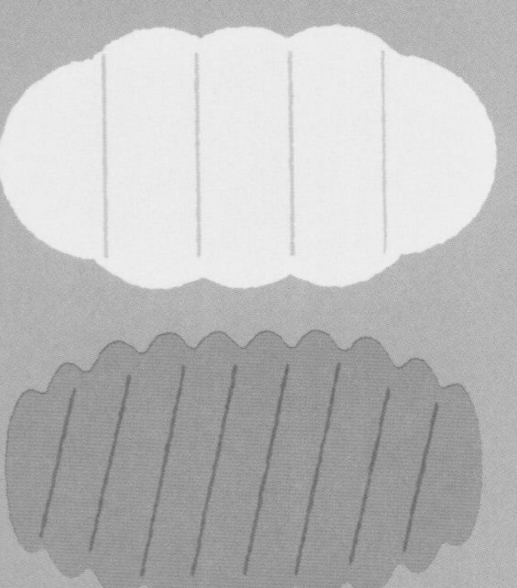

LONG 29

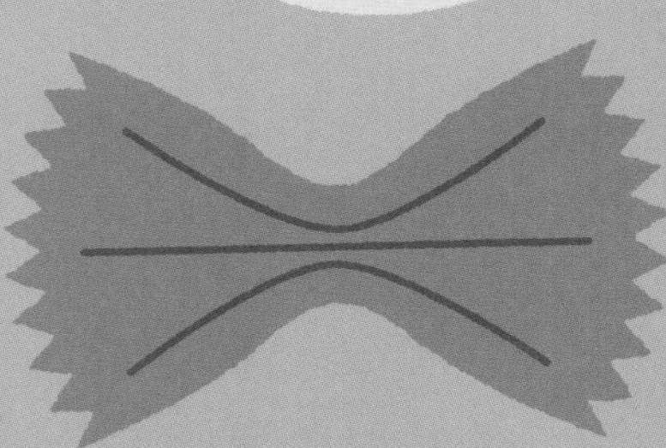

SHORT 89

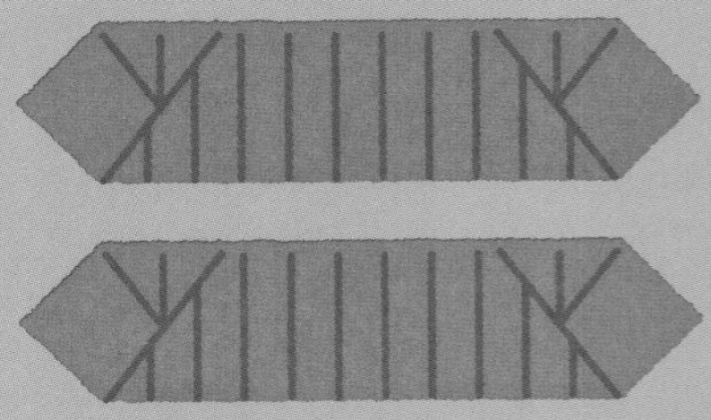

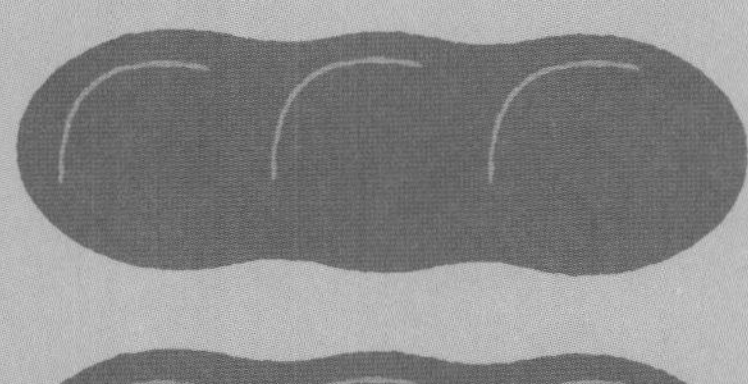

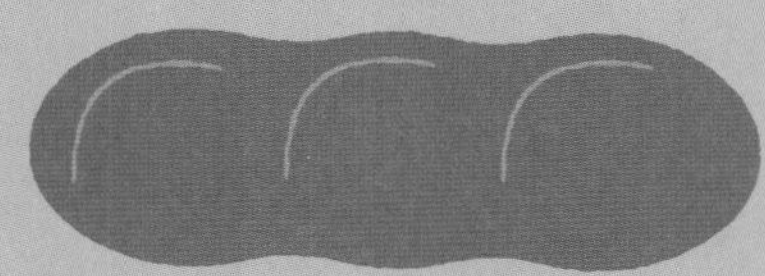

FROM BACK Alec, Elio and Aldo

Introduction

My earliest memories of making pasta are so distant and fragmented that it's hard to say where it all began: being pushed down the road in my pram to collect fresh eggs and cheese; being trusted to sprinkle the flour and eventually even crank the handle on the machine. Or perhaps it was just standing next to Nonna for hours at a time, studying her wrinkled and practised hands as we made countless trays of pasta together for the whole family. Yes, we even all gathered around on milk crates in the driveway once a year, elbow-deep in tomatoes.

I spent many of my youngest years at Nonna's house like this: learning how dough worked, how you can't rush a sugo, and how loud old Italians are. More than that though, I learned an appreciation for life through food. For us, making and sharing pasta carries the memories of a young family making a start in a new country, and the history that they brought with them. It ties together the earliest memories that I have of my grandparents, uncles, aunties, cousins; people who are no longer around for an after-school dinner. It grounds us.

It's also something that I took for granted and forgot about for 20 years. That is, I kept making and eating pasta every weekend, but never considered what it really meant to me. Those meals, seated around Nonna's long table covered with a white tablecloth, surrounded by four generations of family in the quiet foothills of Perth, slipped unremarkably into the past.

Pasta et Al, our blog, began as a way to try and reclaim this part of myself: a sudden realisation that, with my own kids on the way, I needed to pass on our little tradition, and record it. However, as our blog grew, an incredible community began to grow with us. It became clear that a food tradition doesn't need hundreds of years behind it and, in fact, building a new tradition may just be the bit of mindfulness that we all need in our lives right now.

So, this book is about pasta, our way. You'll find many of our old family recipes, loyal to Nonna, but you'll also find playfulness and creativity. We want to show you how to make pasta – a wide and exciting array of it – but we also want to help you dream, embracing and nurturing a true love for the simple things. Starting with flour and eggs.

Our chapters are divided into Long, Short, Big and Flat, Small and Squishy, and Filled; this way you can start broad and then narrow it down to a specific shape. Sixty recipes are split across forty-two types of pasta, each paired with one or two sauces, and, as you read through the book, you'll find an in-depth tutorial preceding every new shape or technique. We've also thrown in a few stories, because food is nothing without the life that surrounds it. And also, because I just couldn't help myself.

Wherever possible, I've included variations, substitutions and alternative pairings. The eighteen dough recipes extend to over thirty when you include flavourings that don't significantly change the overall process, and many are interchangeable. Our introductory chapters on ingredients, equipment and techniques will assist you in mastering these recipes and then extending yourself well beyond the limitations of this book, just as Nonna would have wanted.

Life continues to present all kinds of intensely beautiful moments, while snatching so many others away. And so, as I return home now to finish this book, after almost fifteen years in a different time zone from my extended family, many of them are no longer here to greet me.

Perhaps, like pasta, the best that we can do is to look fondly to the past, and then build something of our own from what we find. Because through it all, sitting down to a plate of fresh pasta every Sunday with my new little family, I can honestly say that these pasta days are the happiest of my life. I hope that this book brings a little simple happiness into your kitchen.

Al.

Ingredients

FLOUR

We make pasta with all kinds of flour and flavour to better complement the shape of the pasta or the sauce – and also just for fun. The secret to successful experimentation, though, is to understand the key variables of a flour's relative gluten strength, protein levels and elasticity when formed into a dough.

Classically, pasta is made with 00 flour: a finer flour with comparatively lower protein and strength than, say, semolina, but greater elasticity. You'll notice that we don't use pure 00 in our doughs, and this is due solely to personal preference for a firmer and less stretchy pasta. Also, because Nonna only ever had access to plain (all-purpose) flour!

We do, however, often mix a little semolina flour into 00 flour to make a dough of greater protein and strength. Really all this does is bring it closer to the properties of plain flour. So, in a pinch, plain will do a decent job.

By contrast, you'll see that some of our doughs are made with strong flour (also often called baker's flour or bread flour). This is the opposite end of the spectrum to 00, with a comparatively high protein percentage, strength and elasticity. This makes it perfect for when you need more resistance as you form your shapes but still want a silky pasta. To bring that elasticity down, changing the texture of the dough, you might replace some of the strong flour with wholemeal (whole-wheat).

Beyond this, you do have all kinds of other flours to consider more from a flavour or even nutritional point of view, such as spelt, rye, cake, stone-ground; and, of course, an endless array of non-flour additions, like vegetable and cocoa powders.

Start simple, learn how to feel your way to an excellent dough, and then experiment.

WATER

Really, this refers to moisture, whether it's from water, eggs, wine, purées, or the humidity in the air. Our recipes can't predict how big your eggs are, or how dry your kitchen is, but they provide a starting point and some tips to guide you.

If the dough is too dry as you mix it, run your hands quickly under the tap; too wet, add a sprinkle of flour. If your pasta sheets are too dry, give them a gentle spritz of water or seal them in plastic wrap. Likewise, air-dry a tacky sheet for a few minutes instead of burying it in flour. Many pasta makers refer to their water in percentages relative to the flour, which is a more accurate measure but can limit how well you get to know your dough. Work through our tutorials and recipes and it will become second nature in no time.

And don't forget: water retained from cooking the pasta is your friend. Its starchy goodness will help thin out an over-reduced sauce, and assist it in binding to your pasta.

EGGS

Pick the best: free-range and raised on spacious land. The simpler you cook, the more important every ingredient becomes. For many pasta doughs, it's mostly flour and eggs, so you will taste the difference. Plus, think of all those happy little chooks.

Technically, remember that eggs are protein and water (and fat, in the yolk), for the purposes of pasta. For example, a yolk only dough will require a whole lot more eggs than a whole egg dough (to make up the required moisture content, given egg whites are largely water), and it may also break more easily (due to the higher protein percentage causing it to be brittle).

We use large eggs in our doughs but, as egg sizes vary wildly, I encourage you to work with the dough and adjust the moisture as needed; see Water, previous column.

EXTRA-VIRGIN OLIVE OIL

We use extra virgin for everything and, like eggs, it's an ingredient to be honoured. Whether it's a dash in your dough, a glug to fry with or a finishing splash on top, pick the best.

SALT

Adding a little finely ground salt to your dough will strengthen the gluten bonds. This is neither good nor bad, just a consideration. If you want a tougher dough with a bit more bite, throw it in. If you'd like a more delicate pasta, leave it out.

When cooking pasta, it is essential to salt the water. It helps to tighten up otherwise brittle pasta and adds flavour. The water should taste salty.

PLEASE NOTE This book uses 20 ml (¾ fl oz) tablespoons. Cooks using 15 ml (½ fl oz) tablespoons should be mindful of slightly increasing the amount with their tablespoon measurements. Metric cup measurements are used, i.e. 250 ml for 1 cup; in the US a cup is 8 fl oz, just smaller, so American cooks should be generous in their cup measurements. Additionally, the recipes in this book were cooked in a fan-forced or convection oven, so if using a conventional oven increase the temperature by 20°C (35°F).

For accuracy, cup measures are not provided for flour in this book; it is recommended to weigh the flour rather than using cups.

Equipment

PASTA BOARD ①

A solid wooden board or benchtop really is the best work surface for making pasta on. It's usefully tactile, and makes it easier to manage moisture (if you need it a little tackier to grip your pasta, or drier to prevent it sticking). A stone surface can be handy for kneading, but takes a lot of flour to prevent the dough sticking once you begin forming sheets and shaping.

BENCH SCRAPER ②

A butter knife was Nonna's weapon of choice, but a solid, straight-edged bench scraper is the more conventional implement these days. Bench scrapers are mostly used for scraping the dough together as it's mixed before kneading, but they also come in handy as a chopping edge when dividing dough.

PASTA MACHINE, OR MATTARELLO ③

Do yourself a favour and choose a reputable brand of machine, as nothing will spoil your pasta experience more than having to battle with a cheap and dodgy roller. We use mainly manual (hand-cranked) machines, although we do have a few excellent stand-mixer attachments to handle those bigger batches. If nothing else, look for a machine with a smooth handle motion and a solid build.

For the purists out there, a mattarello (or very long rolling pin) will do all that a machine can, although it comes with a slightly different skillset. This book is primarily aimed at pasta machine users, if for no other reason than it's how my nonna did it.

PASTRY CUTTERS ④

There are so many out there to choose from, but if I had to pick one it would be the classic zigzag pastry cutter (although a straight-edge cutter is another versatile option). If it takes your fancy, there's also a whole world of beautiful, ornate handcrafted cutters to choose from, but they're obviously not essential.

Apart from that, a high-quality adjustable pasta bike is an incredibly handy tool to have, particularly when cutting squares.

SKEWERS, DOWELS, FERRETTI ⑤

As you work your way through this book and build your experience making pasta, you will no doubt collect an array of long, skinny things to form pasta with. Some pasta will demand dowels of a specific diameter, but for others a skewer will do. Traditional brass ferretti are unexpectedly pleasing tools to work with, but yes, if pressed, you can snip the straight edge out of a coat hanger instead.

RAVIOLI MOULDS ⑥

There's a wide variety of ravioli moulds out there, as well as stamps and even rolling pins. We prefer the open-bottomed type for regular ravs, and are partial to an ornate mould for the big ones.

EXTRUDER ⑦

We use a relatively inexpensive stand-mixer attachment for our extruded pasta (noting that mixer attachments also require the initial investment in a mixer). It's really only suitable for small batches of pasta, but can produce solid results with the right handling. Manual benchtop machines also offer a good price point for what you can do with them, aimed at that same small-batch application. From there, your options range up to professional grade and bronze-plated machines (the latter of which produce a famously rough texture). As this book only includes a few extruded recipes for completeness, we won't linger on extruding.

GNOCCHI BOARD, PETTINE, CAVAROLE ⑧

There are a variety of surfaces suitable for rolling pasta across. Generally, it's done for texture and enhancing the pasta's sauce-holding ability, but it can also be purely for looks. A gnocchi board is obviously useful for ridged gnocchi, but will also come in handy for malloreddus (also known as gnocchetti sardi; see page 142), and to close and shape garganelli (see page 92). A pettine (pasta comb) is the more traditional option for garganelli, producing ridges more closely spaced than a gnocchi board, and cavarole are the most ornate, suitable for anything you feel like rolling across or stamping onto them. None of these are essential, although a gnocchi board is highly recommended. If you get stuck, the kitchen offers numerous substitutes, from the back of grating planes to the seats of wicker chairs (so I've heard ...).

CHITARRA ⑨

This rather niche wooden tool produces one of my favourite pasta types, with a uniquely square edge and chunky cut. It's not a must-have, but you won't regret adding it to your collection.

COOKIE CUTTERS ⑩

While a pasta bike will sort you out for squares, round cookie cutters are the way to go for any circle-based pasta shapes. There are, of course, endless options beyond circle cutters, but they have limited (mostly ravioli) application.

PIPING BAGS, WITH SMALL–MEDIUM TIPS ⑪

Nonna mostly stuck to a teaspoon and her hands, but I tend to use a piping bag for my filled pasta. You'll still need to go old school for chunkier ingredients, but it's much quicker and neater for any smooth fillings. You can make do with a piping bag with the end snipped off, but my preference is to use a medium round tip.

POTATO RICER

Here's one for the gnocchi and potato fillings. You can rub your potatoes through a sieve, but a few passes through the ricer makes for far quicker and easier work.

3
imperia
5
8
8
3
6
6
4
3
8
2
7
4
10
11

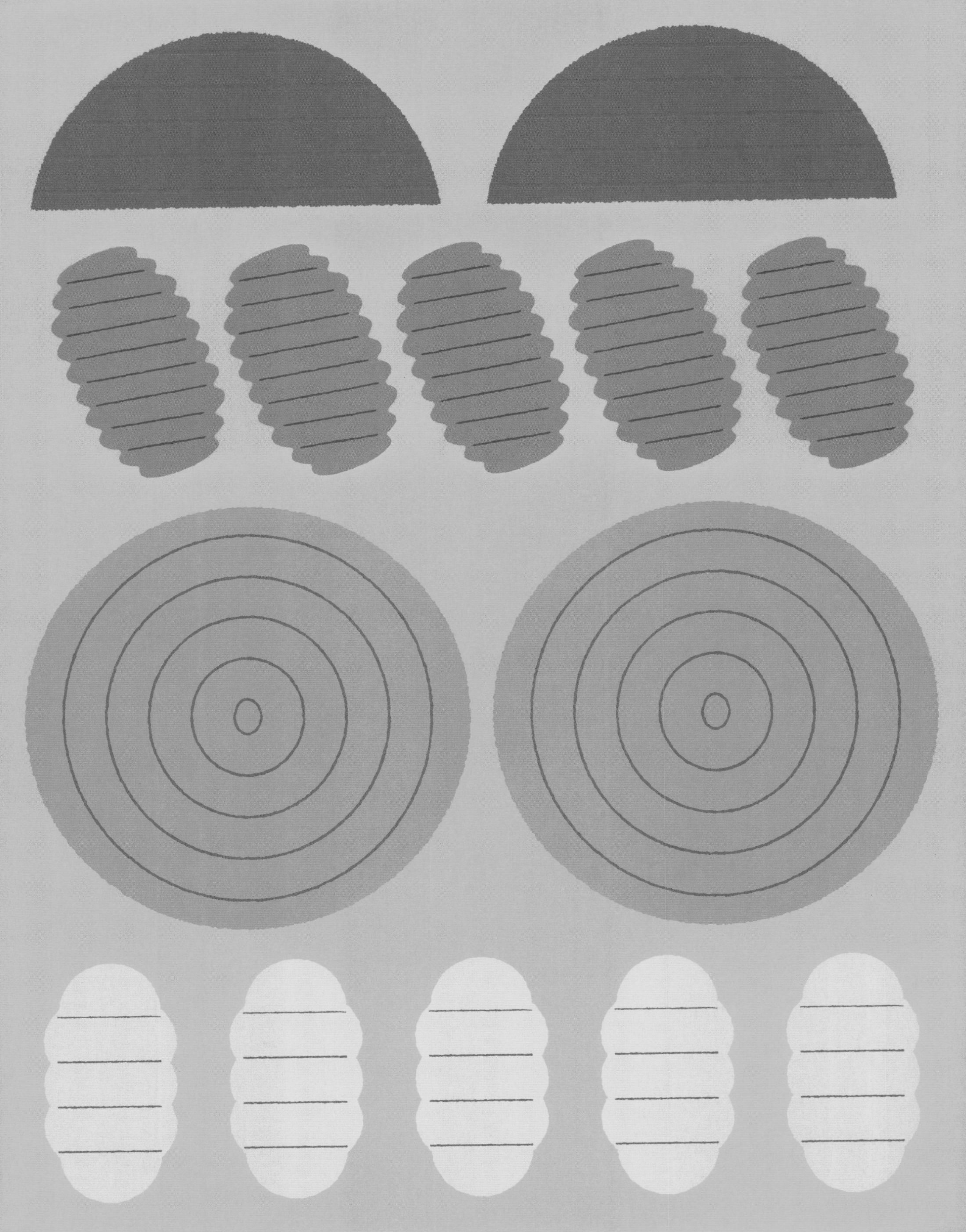

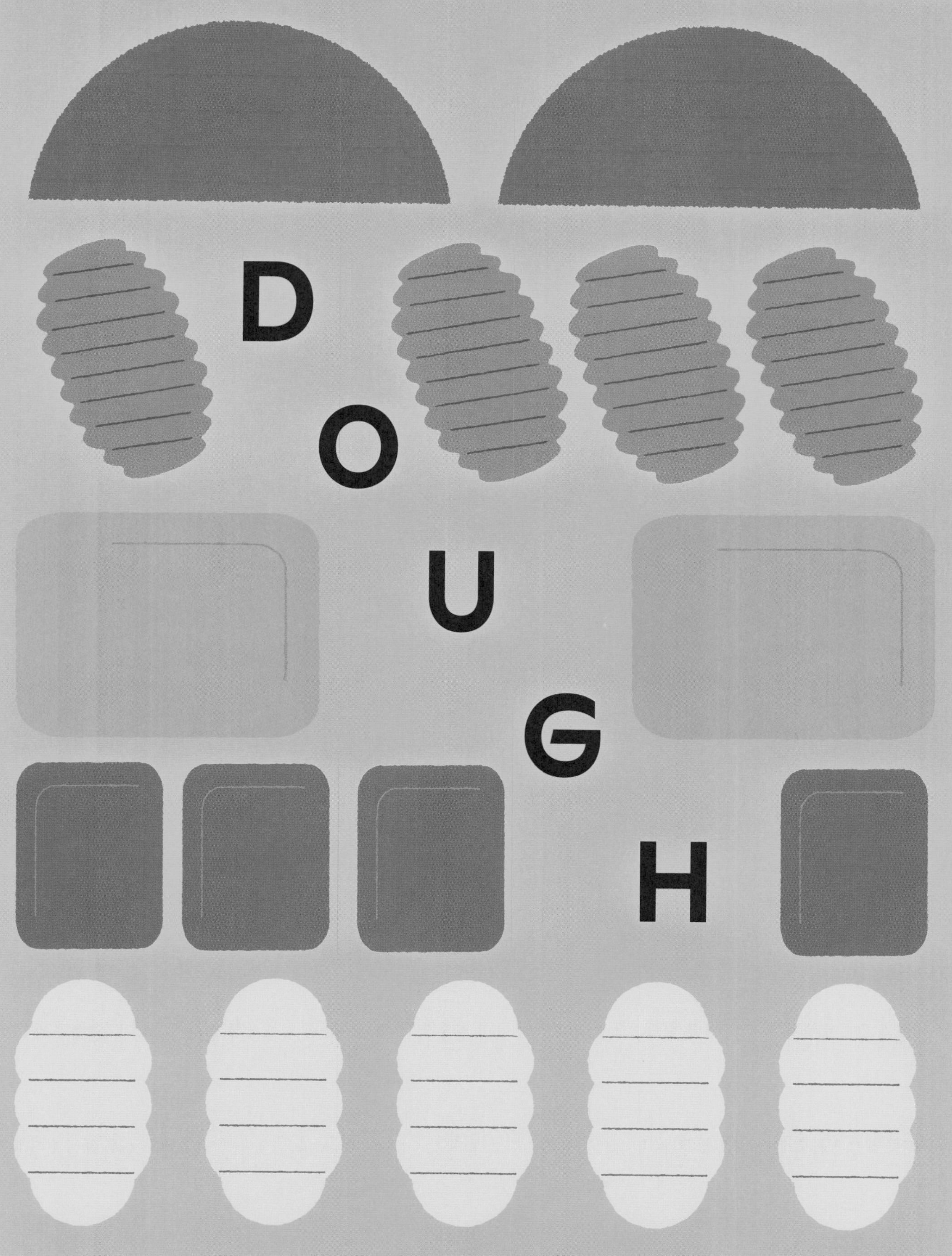
D
O
U
G
H

The doughs that you create are limited only by your imagination, after maybe a brief study of the classics. Fortunately, for pasta, 'the classics' are really 100 g (3½ oz) flour to 1 egg. All of our dough recipes have begun here, with the ingredients then endlessly added to and tinkered with to suit the pasta and the dish. And, of course, adjusted through curious experimentation, improvisation, error or good old-fashioned laziness.

This book is built around the most dependable and versatile of those recipes, the ones we keep coming back to: four plain egg doughs, three plain eggless doughs, and one each of extruded, gnocchi and gnudi doughs. Building on this, there are also twenty-eight variations, ranging from the simple addition of a little powdered ingredient through to stand-alone recipes with more involved modification.

Within this chapter you'll find the ingredient lists for all of the above, as well as introductory tutorials for basic pasta dough and our gluten-free egg dough. All other tutorials reference the dough recipes laid out here, but are themselves found throughout the book, preceding the relevant pasta shapes and styles. Note that cooking times in the final recipes do not include dough preparation and resting.

Read, practise, enjoy, practise.

Basic pasta dough

Every pasta in this book, aside from gluten-free dough (see Tutorial, page 48), extruded shapes (see Tutorial, page 82), and the tenuously classified gnocchi (see Tutorial, page 163), starts with the process described here.

1 Begin by forming a well out of your dry ingredients, either on a clean benchtop, or in a large mixing bowl. I often use the underside of a bowl to press down and hollow out the well's centre. Place all wet ingredients into the centre.

2 Use a fork or your fingers to stir, gradually incorporating the flour until you're left with a shaggy ball. A bench scraper is particularly handy for keeping it all together at this stage. If your dough is too wet, add flour one tablespoon at a time; if too dry, run your hands under the tap and knead in the extra moisture.

3 Once your dough holds together without sticking to your hands or work surface, knead it vigorously for 10 minutes. I find that it turns softer and silkier at around 7 minutes, but throw in an extra three to be sure. To knead, stretch the dough down and away from you with the heel of your hand, before folding it back over itself and repeating. Rotate it occasionally to avoid it stretching out too long.

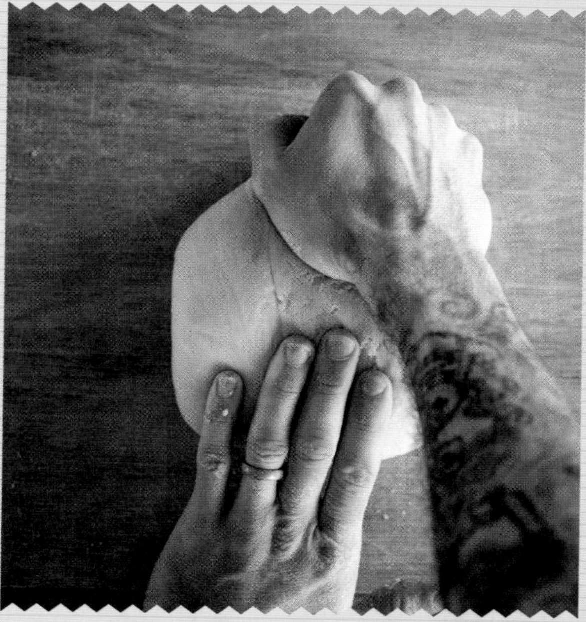

4 After 10 minutes of pummelling that dough like Nonna, flatten it slightly into a thick disc and seal tightly in plastic wrap. Rest (yourself, and the dough) for 30 minutes away from heat or direct sunlight before moving on.

Egg Dough

Almost every egg pasta in this book could be made with the old-fashioned recipe of 100 g (3½ oz) flour to one egg, per person. In fact, this is where they all began, and it remains a perfectly viable option if you're pressed for ingredients. That said, the more that you experiment and tinker, the more you'll notice the difference that flour substitutions, egg ratios and even a little oil can make.

Note that if using these doughs for filled pasta, you can decrease the ingredients by around one-quarter if you want to. We tend to just knead up a full serve and then stuff pasta until we run out of filling, cutting any remaining dough into bonus unfilled shapes.

SERVES 4

WHOLE EGG DOUGH

- 250 g (9 oz) plain (all-purpose) flour
- 150 g (5½ oz) 00 flour
- 4 eggs
- 1 tablespoon extra-virgin olive oil
- ½ teaspoon salt

For a wholemeal variation, use 2 parts plain (all-purpose) flour, to 1 part wholemeal (whole-wheat).

EGG YOLK DOUGH

- 360 g (12½ oz) 00 flour
- 100 g (3½ oz) durum semolina flour
- 18 egg yolks
- 2 tablespoons water
- 2 teaspoons extra-virgin olive oil

No, that's not a mistake: eighteen egg yolks.

WHOLE EGG AND EGG YOLK DOUGH

- 320 g (11½ oz) 00 flour
- 80 g (2¾ oz) durum semolina flour
- 3 eggs
- 3 egg yolks
- 1 teaspoon extra-virgin olive oil
- ½ teaspoon salt

GLUTEN-FREE EGG DOUGH

- 400 g (14 oz) plain (all-purpose) gluten-free flour
- 4 eggs
- 80 ml (2½ fl oz/⅓ cup) water
- 3 teaspoons xanthan gum
- splash of olive oil
- pinch of salt

See Gluten-free dough: Tutorial, page 48.

Variations: Whole egg dough

This is a collection of our main variations on whole egg dough (including whole egg and egg yolk), as found in the recipes and notes throughout the book. When adding dry ingredients, subtract equal amounts of durum semolina flour or plain (all-purpose) flour. For additions of a tablespoon or less, a splash of water may suffice in balancing the moisture.

Note that nettle, red wine, spinach, squid ink, tomato, and wild olive doughs are detailed further on page 24 as separate recipes.

LEMON

- 1 tablespoon lemon juice
- grated zest of 1 lemon

COCOA

- 80 g (2¾ oz) dark cocoa powder

CHLORELLA

- 1 tablespoon chlorella, powdered

SPELT

- 80 g (2¾ oz) spelt flour, regular/ wholemeal (whole-wheat)

HERBS, FRESH, MIXED

- 2 tablespoons parsley, finely chopped
- 2 tablespoons sage, finely chopped
- 2 tablespoons rosemary, finely chopped
- 2 tablespoons thyme, finely chopped

CRACKED PEPPER

- 1 tablespoon black pepper, freshly cracked

SPIRULINA

- 1 tablespoon green or blue spirulina, powdered

Double the amount of blue spirulina for a richer colour.

Variations: Egg yolk dough

Some of these variations are made with wet ingredients; simply replace equal amounts of water with the relevant ingredients, noting the extra instruction for butterfly pea flower dough.

NOTE All variations listed for whole egg dough (and whole egg and egg yolk dough) can be used with gluten-free egg dough, substituting dry additions for gluten-free flour where applicable.

BEETROOT (BEET)

- 2 tablespoons freeze-dried beetroot, powdered

PAPRIKA

- 1½ tablespoons sweet paprika, ground

SALTBUSH

- 1 tablespoon dried saltbush, ground

RYE

- 80 g (2¾ oz) rye flour, light or dark

ANISETTE

- 2 tablespoons Anisette liqueur

Substitute for 2 tablespoons water

BUTTERFLY PEA FLOWER

- 20 g (¾ oz) butterfly pea flower, dried, steeped in 90 ml (3 fl oz) hot water for 5 minutes. Strain well and allow to cool before using.
- ½ teaspoon citric acid (resist the urge to add more, as it will weaken the gluten bonds)

Substitute for 9 of the egg yolks and 2 tablespoons water.

To create two colours of dough, add the citric acid to half of the butterfly pea flower liquid to change it from a blue to magenta colour, before mixing it into the flour. This will then become a soft purple when mixed into the dough.

LEMON AND POPPY SEED

- 2 tablespoons lemon juice
- 1 tablespoon poppy seeds

Substitute for 2 tablespoons water

Eggless dough

SERVES 4

SEMOLINA DOUGH

- 440 g (15½ oz) semolina
- 240 ml (8 fl oz) warm water
- 2 teaspoons extra-virgin olive oil
- 1 teaspoon salt

00 AND SEMOLINA DOUGH

- 240 g (8½ oz) 00 flour
- 120 g (4½ oz) semolina
- 220 ml (7½ fl oz) warm water

Variations: Eggless dough

SAFFRON

- 1 teaspoon saffron threads

Soak in the water for the dough for 10 minutes before mixing all the dough ingredients together.

CRACKED PEPPER

- 1 tablespoon freshly cracked black pepper

Mix well into the other dry dough ingredients.

SUMAC

- 2 tablespoons ground sumac

Mix well into the other dry dough ingredients.

RED WINE DOUGH

- 300 g (10½ oz) strong flour
- 1 tablespoon extra-virgin olive oil
- 360 ml (12 fl oz) red wine, reduced to 120 ml (4 fl oz)

STRONG FLOUR DOUGH

- 300 g (10½ oz) strong flour
- 60 g (2 oz) semolina
- 1 tablespoon extra-virgin olive oil
- 220 ml (7½ fl oz) water, plus more if required

PEPPERMINT GUM

- 2 teaspoons ground peppermint gum

Mix well into the other dry dough ingredients.

WATTLESEED

- 1 tablespoon ground wattleseed

Mix well into the other dry dough ingredients.

SPINACH

- 200 g (7 oz/4 cups) fresh baby spinach leaves, blanched, thoroughly drained and puréed (after blanching, this will reduce to around 90 g/3 oz, so substitute accordingly if using frozen spinach)

Measure the water for the dough on top of the spinach, i.e. you want a wet ingredient total, including the spinach, that's equal in volume to the original water measure.

Flavoured and coloured egg dough

SERVES 4

TOMATO DOUGH

- 200 g (7 oz) 00 flour
- 100 g (3½ oz) durum semolina flour
- 2 eggs
- 100 g (3½ oz) double-strength tomato paste (concentrated purée)
- 1 teaspoon extra-virgin olive oil
- ½ teaspoon salt

NETTLE DOUGH

- 200 g (7 oz) 00 flour
- 80 g (2¾ oz) semolina
- 80 g (2¾ oz) light rye flour
- 160 g (5½ oz) nettles
- 2 eggs
- ½ teaspoon salt

NOTE Nettle requires some special handling. Use a pair of thick gloves to pick the leaves from the very tops of the nettle plants (these will be the newer, softer leaves), and be sure to boil them in water for 2–3 minutes to neutralise the sting. Then drain and purée. For a fun variation, try adding ½ teaspoon of liquid hickory smoke.

RED WINE DOUGH

- 400 g (14 oz) plain (all-purpose) flour
- 4 egg yolks
- 640 ml (21½ fl oz) red wine, reduced to one-quarter of its volume so that you are left with 160 ml (5½ fl oz)

SPINACH DOUGH

- 260 g (9 oz) 00 flour, plus up to another 80 g (2¾ oz) to allow for water left in the spinach
- 140 g (5 oz) durum semolina flour
- 200 g (7 oz/4 cups) fresh baby spinach leaves, blanched, thoroughly drained and puréed (after blanching, this will reduce to around 90 g/3 oz, so substitute accordingly if using frozen spinach)
- 3 eggs
- 1 egg yolk
- 1 tablespoon extra-virgin olive oil
- ½ teaspoon salt

NOTE We're often asked about the colour of our green dough. The trick to a consistent, rich colour is to thoroughly blend the spinach (use an egg or two to help it purée). Additionally, you can chop the whole dough together in a food processor for about 1 minute before kneading.

WILD OLIVE DOUGH

- 360 g (12½ oz) 00 flour
- 220 g (8 oz) durum semolina flour
- 90 g (3 oz) wild black olives, pitted and crushed
- 3 eggs
- 3 egg yolks
- 2 tablespoons extra-virgin olive oil

SQUID INK DOUGH

- 200 g (7 oz) 00 flour
- 200 g (7 oz) durum semolina flour
- 4 eggs
- 1 tablespoon extra-virgin olive oil
- 1 teaspoon squid or cuttlefish ink

Gnocchi and gnudi

SERVES 4

GNOCCHI

- 1.4 kg (3 lb 1 oz) potatoes (floury varieties work best)
- 50 g (1¾ oz) pecorino Romano, grated
- 300 g (10½ oz) 00 flour
- 1 egg

GNUDI

- 350 g (12½ oz) ricotta
- 200 g (7 oz/4 cups) fresh baby spinach leaves, blanched, thoroughly drained and puréed (after blanching, this will reduce to around 90 g/3 oz, so substitute accordingly if using frozen spinach)
- 50 g (1¾ oz) pecorino Romano, grated
- 1 egg yolk
- 2 garlic cloves, crushed
- pinch of nutmeg
- 160 g (5½ oz) semolina (for rolling the gnudi in)

Extruded dough

SERVES 4

EXTRUDED DOUGH

- 2 eggs
- 180 ml (6 fl oz) cold water (see Note)
- 280 g (10 oz) plain (all-purpose) flour
- 280 g (10 oz) semolina
- 1 teaspoon salt

NOTE Our cold water measurement includes the volume of the eggs, so for a four person serve add two eggs to your measuring jug before filling with cold water to the 180 ml (6 fl oz) mark.

For our squid-ink variation, add 1 teaspoon squid or cuttlefish ink.

On remembering the past

Food is a story that we write and tell over and over. It's so primordially tied to who we are as humans that it can't help but attract our histories and identities. With it we remember the past, embrace the present, laugh, cry and look to the future.

My nonna and nonno came to Australia in the fifties, sailing separately into Fremantle aboard the *Sebastiano Caboto* and the *Hellenic Prince*. My nonna had been born in the hills of Calabria three months after her father left for Australia, and so actually met him for the first time on foreign soil over a decade later. She would talk about their uncomfortable first embrace in the port. One of her huge green steamer trunks still sits in my living room. My nonno, from coastal Calabria, adventured out at around the same time as Nonna, without family but in the company of other young men from his town; men he would stay friends with for the rest of his life. He worked hard and, as with so many Italian migrants of that time, sent almost everything that he earned back to Italy.

The life that they eventually built here together was hard, the language unfamiliar, racism brushed off before it could overwhelm them. But they did build a life, and a family, weaving into their new world so many familiar customs and traditions transplanted from Calabria. I guess that when you have few material possessions to carry into a new life, you instead bring with you those little daily rituals that filled your old life. And, of course, amongst and central to all of that was food.

Nonno with his children, Ma closest to him; circa 1967–1968

I was blissfully non-existent for another thirty-something years, as the seeds of a new future grew into a community and, really, a generation. Calabria and Australia blended, 'Italian' diverging and evolving into unique populations of those left behind and those creating a new identity for themselves abroad. I appeared after most of the hard work had been done, but I felt its significance from a young age, standing next to my nonna for hours making pasta, talking, and spending countless evenings around her long table retelling those old tales over a home-cooked meal with the whole family. Pasta is something so simple that it can be taught easily, repeated often and passed across language and culture barriers for generations. Fundamentally unchanged. And so, as I stand there kneading up a sweat every Sunday, I feel it tying me unwaveringly to my past.

That said, one of the greatest things about history – in common with pasta – is that you can make a little bit whenever you like. You don't need to inherit some secret kitchen art, just clear a little bench space and start cooking. Create beautiful moments now, let them grow, and, as you eventually fade into the past, the traditions that you began may just carry the smallest bit of you into the future.

Nonna and Nonno with Ma, outside the Perth General Post Office; 1959

'Pasta is something so simple that it can be taught easily, repeated often and passed across language and culture barriers for generations.'

L
O
N
G

Nonna would have scowled quizzically if I'd ever asked her to list her ingredients by weight. Or by cup measure. Or even by the handful. I often talk about how pasta carries memories with it, but it also works the other way around. Nonna knew her dough by instinct: by look, feel and taste. I remember pasta days beginning with the upending of a bag of flour, and then a choose-your-own-adventure of balancing that with water, eggs, spinach and salt. To this day, whenever I pour out my flour accurate to the gram, first go, I photograph the scales and send it to the family. I rarely get many responses but the favourites album on my phone is filling up nicely.

The first pasta that I usually introduce beginners to – the first that I made with each of my boys, and indeed one of the first that I learned from Nonna – is fettuccine. Long egg pasta in general is a wonderful place to start your pasta journey. Its ingredient list may not be quite as short as the flour and water doughs', but it is more versatile.

The first half of this chapter includes recipes for tagliolini, linguine, fettuccine and pappardelle. These shapes are mostly defined by their increasing widths and various thicknesses, although linguine have a characteristic rounded edge. All can be cut by hand or machine. Spaghetti alla chitarra, which also features, uses a specialised piece of equipment to cut crisp, blocky edges. This chitarra will generally have narrower strings on one side and wider on the other, allowing for two width options.

Up until the point of choosing a final thickness and cutting into ribbons, the dough preparation for all of these shapes is the same. It also forms the basis of most pasta featured in this book. Master a sheet of basic egg dough and you've unlocked the key to almost every form of fresh pasta out there.

Finally, this chapter also includes busiate, pici, gemelli, lorighittas, fileja and extruded pasta. Related only by their length, these eggless pasta shapes (with the exception of our extruded varieties) introduce simple shaping into the pasta-making process.

TUTORIAL

Handmade pasta

The basics, the classics, the pasta that you'll always come back to.

1 Begin with your choice of well-kneaded and rested egg dough (see Basic pasta dough: Tutorial, page 16). If you're game, or have only a small amount of dough to work with, flatten it out enough to fit into the thickest pasta machine setting. For everyone else, cut the dough into roughly one-person portions and seal all but the piece you're about to use in plastic wrap. This will prevent it drying out while you're hitting social media with progress shots or putting out toddler spot-fires at the other end of the house.

2 Roll the dough through the thickest setting on the machine a few times, folding it over itself in between passes. It should take on a more consistent texture after a few repetitions. Many people add more flour at this stage if the dough is too wet, but I prefer to lay it out on the pasta board for a few minutes, regularly checking how much it stretches and sticks. Any non-semolina flour that you add to the outside of a sheet will help it pass through the machine, but will also likely stay there, turning your cooked pasta a little gluggy. Semolina is a better choice to prevent pasta sticking to itself, but won't help if your dough is more than a little tacky. Learning to control the moisture levels in your pasta by harnessing the elements is a more thoughtful approach, and basically a minor superpower attainable to the home cook (see Water, page 9).

3 Incrementally step through the settings on your machine, thick to narrow, until you reach the desired thickness for your pasta. I'm going to be bold and say that this is ultimately a personal preference. Nonna always went thicker, and so I tend to do the same.

4 Cut the sheets to length, and then form your individual strands of pasta. Turn the page for a little cheat sheet of approximate traditional dimensions. Approximate, because pasta specifications are 10 per cent standardised and 90 per cent impassioned and divided opinion.

Pasta made with the chitarra is a little different, as thick as it is wide (at least for the more traditional spaghetti spacing). Form your sheets to length, dust them well with semolina, and then lay them along the strings. Make sure that you leave space at each end, as it will stretch. Roll and gently drag a pin back and forth along the wires until the spaghetti drops through into the tray below. Tip the chitarra on its side to collect your freshly cut pasta.

PASTA	THICKNESS	LENGTH	WIDTH
PAPPARDELLE	0.5 mm (1⁄32 in)	20–25 cm (8–10 in)	2–3 cm (¾ in– 1¼ in)
TAGLIOLINI	0.8 mm (1⁄16 in)	25–30 cm (10–12 in)	2 mm (⅛ in)
FETTUCCINE	1 mm (1⁄16 in)	25–30 cm (10–12 in)	1 cm (½ in)
LINGUINE	2 mm (⅛ in)	25–30 cm (10–12 in)	4 mm (3⁄16 in)
SPAGHETTI ALLA CHITARRA	3 mm (⅛ in)	25–30 cm (10–12 in)	3 mm (⅛ in)
FETTUCCINE ALLA CHITARRA	3 mm (⅛ in)	25–30 cm (10–12 in)	5 mm (¼ in)

Finally, all of these shapes can be rolled with a pin and cut by hand. Once your sheets are ready, simply coat well with semolina, and then fold in half, thirds or quarters before chopping into appropriately wide strips; unfold and shake loose. Note that hand-cutting benefits from slightly drier sheets of dough to avoid it sticking to itself when folded.

A NOTE ON DRYING AND STORING PASTA

For long pasta, neat little nests do work in the very short term (eating the same day), but you need to be confident that there's not too much moisture in your dough, and that the pasta is well coated in semolina to prevent it from sticking together. Using semolina instead of regular flour to dust the pasta will prevent it from becoming too stodgy when cooked, as the semolina will sink to the bottom of the pot.

A safer alternative to nests, if you're uncertain, is to simply toss the pasta in semolina and spread it out thinly on a wooden board or baking paper. If you're cooking it the same day, leave it to air-dry for 3–6 hours, otherwise refrigerate it uncovered (this will aid its dehydration and give it a little extra bite when cooked).

The amount of time that you dry your pasta will vary depending on the shape and the climate. You want it dry enough to no longer be tacky, but not so dry that it breaks when handled. Similarly, for filled pasta, ensure that the undersides are well dusted, and spread them out on baking paper in the fridge. Eat pasta stored like this within 1–2 days.

Freezing pasta is another perfectly good option. No joke, Nonna had a freezer dedicated to pasta. Just make sure that it still has a good coating of semolina, and that you freeze it all spread out in a single layer before combining it into smaller, more convenient bags or containers for longer-term freezing. If sealed properly, it should last for 3–6 months. Note that cheese fillings may become more granular in texture when frozen, but are still fine to eat.

Pasta in our family rarely hangs around long enough for us to have any real opinion on dehydrators, but by all means give it a shot. True dehydration will give your pasta a more pronounced, al dente bite.

Tagliolini aglio e olio

SERVES 4 | TOTAL TIME 20 MINS

My ma, when she was very young, would wait for her chance to slip unobserved into the kitchen, secretly pour herself half a coffee cup of olive oil, and then hide it away deep inside the bread cupboard. She'd then seize opportunities throughout the day to sneak back in and pinch pieces of crusty bread to dip in her oil. The danger attached to such an innocent snack might not seem immediately obvious to younger generations, but Southern Italian nonnas, to their own kids, are not the eternally forgiving pushovers known to their grandchildren and, by virtue, much of the wider world. The same Nonna leaping to my defence against an undoubtedly well-deserved telling-off from my ma (usually for talking back or straight up swearing) only one generation earlier would have been flying across the room, wooden spoon or shoe aloft, flames licking at the ceiling, over a little stray oil.

So, when you next choose your olive oil, make sure that it's good enough to have you tiptoeing past a vigilant and wrathful old Italian in a complex plan of juvenile deception. And then keep it in a cool, dark place, ready to save dinner when all that you have supplies or time for is aglio e olio.

- 1 × quantity Whole egg dough (page 18)
- 6–8 garlic cloves, finely chopped
- 120 ml (4 fl oz) extra-virgin olive oil
- dried chilli flakes, to taste
- 1 small handful of parsley, finely chopped
- salt and pepper, to taste

Form the dough into sheets and cut into tagliolini of around 1 mm (1⁄16 in) thickness (see Handmade pasta: Tutorial, page 33). Cook in a large pot of lightly salted water for 2–3 minutes until firm to bite but with no raw dough showing when cut into. Drain, reserving 200 ml (7 fl oz) pasta water.

Gently fry the garlic in the oil over a medium heat, stirring, for 4–5 minutes; it should be soft but not browning. Stir in the chilli flakes to taste, and then use tongs to drop the pasta directly into the pan from the pot. Add the reserved pasta water and stir well but gently for 2–3 minutes. The sauce should emulsify and cling to the pasta.

Toss in the parsley, season to taste and serve.

ON PASTA

Often, a more robust pasta like spaghetti is paired with this traditional Neapolitan sauce, but you'd be hard-pressed to find a pasta that doesn't work with good old olive oil and garlic. When using tagliolini like this, just roll it a little thicker, cut your garlic a little finer, and toss it all together with a little more care.

ON INGREDIENTS

Never accept a cookbook's recommendation on garlic. Even this cookbook. Those of us who spend more time peeling garlic than sautéing it know what I'm talking about. Double it, triple it, throw whole bulbs in with reckless abandon. I'm just not bold enough to write that in the ingredients list.

For an extra fresh taste, warm the oil and let your finely chopped garlic soak in it for a few minutes instead of cooking.

Saltbush spaghetti alla chitarra with whitebait

SERVES 4 | TOTAL TIME 30 MINS

I'm not going to lie and say that I would have gone near whitebait as a child. I was like a small fishy-fish detector, sniffing out the zeppole with anchovies in them and fleeing at the sound of a sardine tin peeling open. I can safely say that I've come around. So much so that this recipe includes garum, a Roman fish sauce traditionally made by fermenting a mix of salted fish guts in the sun for a few months. Don't let that throw you off though; it brings a deep, subtle umami to anything that it's added to, and food preservation has come a long way.

This dish also includes fefferoni. I am mad about these little yellow chillies. They're one of the most familiar flavours from my childhood, and I could have cried at the smell as they hit the pan. In fact, we all cried a bit, and the rest of the family had to evacuate as the lower floor was enveloped by a cloud of stovetop pepper spray. Fefferoni: available in hot *and* mild.

- 1 × quantity Whole egg dough (page 18), made with half 00 flour, half durum semolina flour and 1 tablespoon finely powdered saltbush (see page 21)
- 120 ml (4 fl oz) extra-virgin olive oil, plus a generous splash to serve
- 200 g (7 oz) fresh whitebait or silver fish
- 2 tablespoons 00 flour, or whatever flour you have left from making the pasta
- 10–12 whole garlic cloves, peeled and lightly smashed under the side of a knife
- 4–6 whole fefferoni chillies
- 160 ml (5½ fl oz) dry white wine
- 1 teaspoon garum (or substitute with fish sauce or minced anchovy fillet)
- lemon juice, to taste
- 2 tablespoons very finely chopped parsley and cracked black pepper, to serve

Prepare the pasta sheets to a thickness of about 3 mm (⅛ in), and cut on the narrowest side of the chitarra (see Handmade pasta: Tutorial, page 33). Dust in semolina and set aside.

Bring a large pot of lightly salted water to the boil over a high heat. Meanwhile, heat the oil in a frying pan over a high heat. Dredge the whitebait in the flour and add to the pan, frying for 30 seconds, or until the fish has turned white and begun to crumble. Remove the fish from the pan and lower the heat to medium.

Add the crushed garlic cloves and whole chillies to the pan and cook, stirring, for 3–4 minutes, or until colour begins to develop. Add the white wine and garum, stir, and cook for a further 2–3 minutes.

While the sauce reduces, drop the pasta into the boiling water and cook for 4–5 minutes before testing for doneness. Drain, retaining half a cup of the pasta water.

Return the heat to high and add the whitebait and pasta with a generous splash of olive oil. Toss thoroughly, gradually adding the pasta water (if required) until the sauce and pasta are completely emulsified. Stir in a squeeze of lemon juice before removing from the heat.

Serve with finely chopped parsley and a crack of black pepper.

ON PASTA

If you don't have a chitarra, cut it by hand or substitute with spaghetti, linguine or fettuccine (see page 34).

ON INGREDIENTS

Saltbush is a fantastic and versatile native Australian ingredient. It's one of those subtle additions that you can throw into a dish for a little extra depth. Here, it brings a hint of salty earth to the fish in the sauce. Just be sure to grind it as finely as possible if adding it to a delicate pasta like tagliolini.

Whitebait can be used to refer to all immature edible fish, but here we're using one particular variety, marketed as silver fish – not those little bugs that would eat Dad's slippers.

Garum may have, in fact, been used outside of Rome as early as the fifth century BCE. My apologies to any Greeks or Phoenicians out there with further information.

Squid ink fettuccine alla chitarra with capsicum and home-made tuna in oil

SERVES 4 | TOTAL TIME 3 HRS 20 MINS

Tuna and capsicum (bell pepper) pasta is a true family classic, a simple and delicious dish that was on regular rotation when I was a kid. It's as straightforward as a couple of capsicums, a tin of tuna and pasta. Despite this simplicity, or perhaps because of it, it makes for an unexpectedly satisfying meal and a perfect option for a quick dinner.

Now there's nothing wrong with using good old tinned fish, but we're suckers for punishment (and home-made food) so we like to make our own tuna in oil. It's not truly preserved, but will last in the fridge for around two weeks before you should get suspicious of it. So, if you come across a good chunk of tuna in your travels, remember this recipe: boil and oil.

1 × quantity Squid ink dough (page 24)

TUNA IN OIL

120 g (4½ oz) salt

400 g (14 oz) tuna steak

240 ml (8 fl oz) extra-virgin olive oil

SAUCE

6 garlic cloves, chopped

2 tablespoons extra-virgin olive oil

1 kg (2 lb 3 oz) red capsicums (bell peppers), cut into thin strips

salt and freshly cracked black pepper, to taste

Use the squid ink dough to prepare pasta sheets 2 mm (⅛ in) in thickness; cut into fettuccine alla chitarra on the wider setting (see Handmade pasta: Tutorial, page 33). Alternatively, cut by machine or hand.

For the tuna in oil, add the salt to 1.5 litres (51 fl oz/6 cups) water in a saucepan and bring to the boil over a high heat. Remove any skin and dark flesh from the tuna, then add to the water. Reduce the heat to low and maintain a gentle simmer for 1.5–2 hours. Remove and drain.

Optional: if you have the time, allow the tuna to cool, then refrigerate overnight. This will ensure that it is completely dry and will firm it up.

Cut the tuna into 3–4 cm (1¼–1½ in) strips and place into clean, dry jars or airtight containers. Fill with oil, ensuring that the tuna is completely submerged. Store sealed and refrigerated for up to 2 weeks.

To make the sauce, gently fry the garlic in the oil in a large frying pan over a low heat for 5–6 minutes. Do not allow to brown. Add the capsicums, season with salt, and stir. Cover the pan and cook for 45 minutes, stirring regularly, until the capsicums are soft and beginning to brown.

Uncover and cook for a further 3–4 minutes, then add the drained tuna, breaking it up slightly as you stir it through. Remove from the heat.

To plate up, cook the pasta in lightly salted water for 6–8 minutes, or until firm but no longer raw, and then drain, retaining a cup of the pasta water. Drop the pasta directly into the frying pan with the sauce and add a little of the pasta water if required to assist emulsification. Serve with a fresh crack of black pepper to taste.

ON PASTA

Though we've paired it here with a squid ink fettuccine, growing up we would usually eat it with just plain fettuccine or spaghetti.

ON INGREDIENTS

Squid ink does impart a true salty, fishy flavour to the pasta, not only colour; be aware if fishiness is not your thing. It also makes a fine mess of wooden pasta boards or unsealed benchtops (though more so in the mixing and kneading stages), so just consider that whilst handling.

Skip the whole tuna bit and save a good 2 hours by substituting with 400 g (14 oz) drained tinned tuna in oil.

Wholemeal fettuccine carbonara

SERVES 4 | TOTAL TIME 20 MINS

I remember eating carbonara in a tiny upstairs osteria somewhere in Rome, twenty-something years ago, harangued by Fabrizio and Lucio singing 'O Sole Mio', as the staff came out from the kitchen to join them. It was such a perfectly joyous moment, having just reunited with distant family and loaded up with carbs, that I bought their album and play it to this day when I'm making pasta, the roar of the rangehood ironing out any minor imperfections.

Carbonara is a dish as fearlessly Roman as my great-uncle 'shortcutting' us through town by taking to the tram tracks in his tiny Fiat Bambino. It too requires a deft hand; a gentle touch is the difference between a velvety, smooth emulsion and scrambled eggs on pasta. A game of chicken, if you will. The heat of the pan, the oncoming tram. Yet master it, and you will have uncovered the great Italian culinary beauty of simplicity with a little finesse. Also, it's very moreish and a crowd-pleaser.

- 1 × quantity Whole egg dough (page 18), made with two-thirds plain (all-purpose) flour, one-third wholemeal (whole-wheat) flour
- 80 g (2¾ oz) prosciutto
- 2 tablespoons extra-virgin olive oil
- 280 g (10 oz) pancetta, chopped into narrow strips (or substitute with guanciale or bacon)
- 4 eggs
- 4 egg yolks
- 100 g (3½ oz) pecorino Romano, grated, plus extra to serve
- salt and freshly cracked black pepper

Form the dough into sheets of around 0.8 mm (1⁄16 in) thickness and cut into fettuccine (see Handmade pasta: Tutorial, page 33).

Fry the prosciutto in the olive oil over a medium–high heat for 2–3 minutes until crispy. Remove to paper towel. Add the pancetta in its place and fry for 5–6 minutes until crunchy.

While the pancetta cooks, boil the fettuccine in a large pot of lightly salted water for 2–3 minutes until cooked through; sit a large metal mixing bowl over the top to warm it while you do this.

In a separate bowl, mix together the eggs, yolks, cheese and some pepper to season. Remove the pancetta pan from the heat and use tongs to drop the cooked fettuccine directly into it from the pot. Transfer to the warmed mixing bowl, pour in the egg and cheese mix, and stir vigorously to avoid clumping. Add a little retained pasta water if the sauce is too dry.

Serve with the crispy prosciutto crumbled on top, extra grated cheese and a crack of pepper.

ON PASTA

Wholemeal (whole-wheat) is really just a preference, giving the pasta a bit of earthiness and depth that I particularly love paired with simpler sauces. You can quite happily swap in any number of other pasta shapes, but longer is probably better. Spaghetti or linguine would be my other picks.

ON INGREDIENTS

Some people use cream in their carbonara. I won't say to avoid cream out of any respect for tradition, but I will ask you to consider it as a matter of self-respect. You're better than cream in carbonara.

A note too for those avoiding raw eggs: they are deliberately undercooked in a carbonara (if you heat the sauce too much it will scramble). If this is you, please ensure that you're cooking with pasteurised eggs, or consider a different sauce altogether.

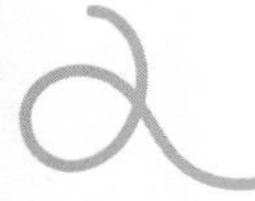

Pappardelle with oxtail and Java long pepper ragù

SERVES 4 | TOTAL TIME 5 HRS 30 MINS

Although the Romans love a bit of oxtail, I actually tried it for the first time in Indonesia, sitting by a rice field just outside of Yogyakarta. It was late, dim lighting barely touching the darkness only metres away, and the humidity was perfectly tempered by bursts of monsoonal rain. I was young and blissfully lost in the depths of a foreign world, with the freedom to leap before I'd finalised the landing. And that simple bowl of sop buntut has stuck in my mind with the clarity that such realisations often lend to those most ordinary of moments.

Back in Australia, my nonna continued to lament the fact that I'd spoken fluent Indonesian from primary school, but only ever understood enough Calabrese to answer back or run when I was in trouble. She'd probably be scowling right now as I recount it in a book ostensibly about pasta. Nonetheless, Indonesia made me feel closer to myself in a way that took me nearly two decades to discover with my own Italian blood.

I wouldn't say that my family ever displayed shame at their heritage, though they had often been made to feel it, but the stories told to the younger generation certainly made it seem like a chapter that had finished when Australia began – so that Australia could begin. We passed a little blindly through an idyllic childhood where the daily mundanities were actually beautiful lingering ties to this past. Dropping by Nonna's for dinner, remembering to return empty sauce bottles for trade-in, and taking home leftovers in a saucepan secured closed with a tea towel.

It sometimes takes a foreign culture to truly see your own, and I think that in this way Indonesia helped me to find what had been right in front of me for all of those years. And so, there's a light touch of Java pepper in this ragù.

- 1 × quantity Whole egg dough (page 18)
- 1 kg (2 lb 3 oz) oxtail
- 40 g (1½ oz) plain (all-purpose) flour
- salt and freshly cracked black pepper, to season
- 80 ml (2½ fl oz/⅓ cup) extra-virgin olive oil
- 4–6 garlic cloves, coarsely chopped
- 1 onion, coarsely chopped
- 1 small carrot, coarsely chopped
- 1 celery stalk, coarsely chopped
- 200 g (7 oz) crushed tomatoes
- 375 ml (12½ fl oz/1½ cups) red wine
- 6 whole Java long peppers
- 2 rosemary sprigs (or substitute with dried rosemary)
- 1 small handful of fresh oregano (or substitute with dried)
- 2 bay leaves
- pinch of sugar

Prepare pasta sheets of 0.5–0.8 mm (1⁄32–1⁄16 in) thickness and cut into pappardelle (see Handmade pasta: Tutorial, page 33).

Preheat the oven to 200°C (390°F). Dredge the oxtail in flour seasoned lightly with salt and pepper, then use 2 tablespoons of the olive oil to brown it in a flameproof casserole over a high heat, 5–6 minutes per side. Remove from the pot.

Remove any burnt (not browned) flour and meat, drop the heat to low, then to the same casserole add the remaining olive oil, along with the garlic, onion, carrot and celery. Cook gently, stirring, for 10–15 minutes until everything softens and begins to brown.

Stir in the tomatoes, wine, Java long peppers and herbs. Season with sugar, salt and pepper, scraping any caught bits off the inside of the pot and into the sauce. Return the oxtail to the pot and add enough water to completely submerge the meat. Cover and transfer to the oven; cook for 4–5 hours.

Lift the bones out of the pot and discard, then break the meat apart with a fork or tongs, stirring it back into the sauce.

Cook the pappardelle in a large pot of salted water for 2–3 minutes, ensuring that it's done, and then drop directly into the sauce, retaining one cup of pasta water. Stir well, coating the pasta thoroughly with sauce. Add a little pasta water if it's too dry.

ON PASTA

As well as other long pasta, this is also a great ragù to pair with short, thick shapes like rigatoni (see page 118).

ON INGREDIENTS

If you prepare this ragù in advance, preferably refrigerating overnight, you will be able to skim off the fat that collects on the surface, if you wish.

Egg yolk pappardelle with mushroom and taleggio sauce

SERVES 4 | TOTAL TIME 45 MINS

One day, when I'm living in a whimsically decrepit villa in southern Italy, backing on to woodlands and looking down towards the ocean, I'll grab my whittled walking stick and amble out the back door to see what mushrooms I can find. Then I'll casually write a recipe about it as I sip thick double espressos and listen to Paganini. But right now, I'm 16,000 kilometres away, and an unaccomplished whittler, so little Al is in charge of fungi.

His love for mushrooms really stems, so to speak, from his earliest walking days when they were all that he could reach at the markets. He still collects them for us every weekend, and thinks it's hilarious to hold a giant portobello to his ear and make phone calls. Which of course it is. The mushrooms in this recipe were chosen based on which varieties provided the clearest reception to call Nonna on, but don't feel limited to this method of selection.

- 1 × quantity Egg yolk dough (page 18)
- 2 garlic bulbs
- 20 g (¾ oz) dried porcini, rehydrated in hot water (drain well and retain the water)
- 800 g (1 lb 12 oz) mixed fresh mushrooms, thinly sliced
- 80 ml (2½ fl oz/⅓ cup) extra-virgin olive oil
- 150 g (5½ oz) taleggio, cubed
- 100 ml (3½ fl oz) full-cream (whole) milk
- salt and freshly cracked black pepper, to taste
- grated Parmigiano Reggiano, to serve

Preheat the oven to 200°C (390°F). Form the dough into sheets of 0.5–0.8 mm (1/32–1/16 in) thickness, and cut into pappardelle (see Handmade pasta: Tutorial, page 33).

Roast the garlic bulbs whole in the oven for 20 minutes. They should brown slightly on the outside. Allow to cool.

Sauté the porcini and fresh mushrooms in the olive oil over a medium heat for about 5 minutes. Remove from the pan and set aside. In the same pan, gently melt the taleggio into the milk over a low heat. Once it has completely melted, add a few tablespoons of porcini water to taste.

Squeeze the roasted garlic out of the cloves and add to the milk and taleggio, along with the sautéed mushrooms. Season with salt and pepper to taste.

Cook the pappardelle for 2–3 minutes in a large pot of salted water, test for doneness, and transfer directly from the pot into the pan, retaining a little pasta water. Toss together thoroughly, adding a little pasta water or porcini water if too dry.

Serve with Parmigiano Reggiano and cracked pepper.

ON PASTA

This is not a light meal, so for a little less decadence, try making your pappardelle with Whole egg dough (page 18). Pasta alternatives range from long to short and hollow, so you may just want to chop your mushrooms chunkier or finer depending on what you choose.

ON INGREDIENTS

If you don't have a toddler handy, you can also select the mushrooms yourself.

Gluten-free pasta

Gluten-free dough is a very different medium to work with, and so deserves its own brief tutorial. The recipe in this book (see page 19) has been tried and tested to perfection, many times and in many applications. I won't pretend that it's an easy dough to work with, but stick with it and you will be able to make both unfilled and filled pasta.

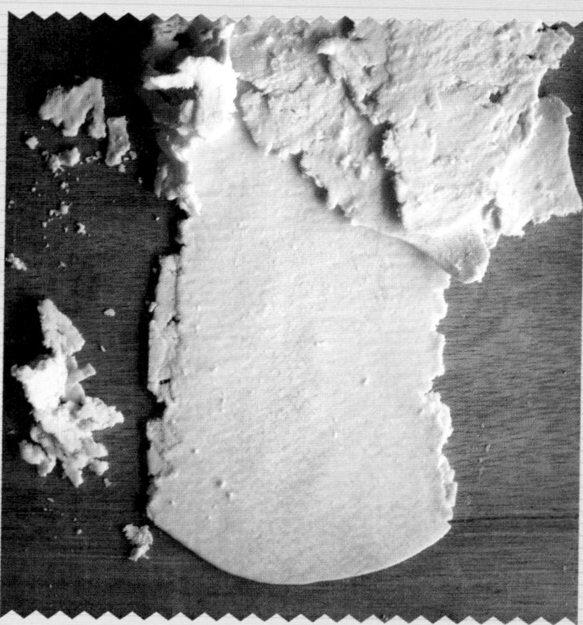

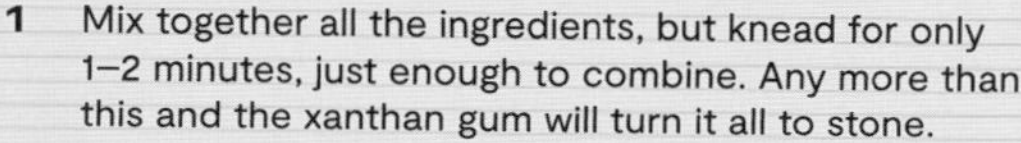

1 Mix together all the ingredients, but knead for only 1–2 minutes, just enough to combine. Any more than this and the xanthan gum will turn it all to stone.

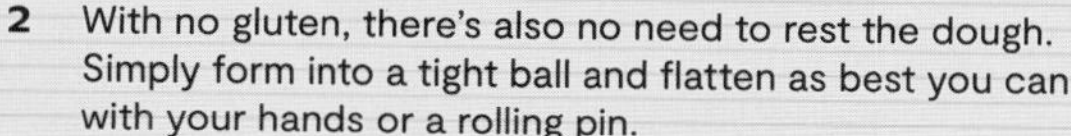

2 With no gluten, there's also no need to rest the dough. Simply form into a tight ball and flatten as best you can with your hands or a rolling pin.

3 Begin feeding the dough through the pasta machine, starting at the thickest setting and working incrementally through to your desired thickness. Expect this to get a bit messy and difficult, but don't give up!

4 When a hole appears, just fold the dough over itself to cover, and then pass it back through on the same setting. You may need multiple passes on the thicker settings before progressing to thinner widths.

5 Cut and fill as required. This dough holds up as a substitute for both unfilled and filled pasta, although it is best suited to long or stamped shapes.

Multi-coloured pasta

The creative colour possibilities that exist with pasta are endless, and would fill a whole book of their own. So instead of providing an exhaustive guide, we're going to show you a few techniques that you can explore for yourself. Throughout the chapters you'll find recipes that call for two-tone lamination, single and double-sided stripes, squiggles, spots, spirals and marbling. These are the techniques that we'll cover now.

TWO-TONE PASTA 

1 Select two egg doughs of different colours and work each into sheets slightly thinner than your final desired pasta thickness (see Basic pasta dough: Tutorial, page 16).

2 Lay one sheet out flat on a lightly floured work surface, spritz lightly with water and lay a sheet of the other colour along the top of it. Be careful to avoid air bubbles. Roll back through the machine on one setting thicker than that used to initially sheet the dough. Cut and shape as required.

SINGLE-SIDED STRIPES AND SQUIGGLES 

1 Select two or more doughs of different colours and work each into sheets approximating the desired thickness of your intended pasta (see Basic pasta dough: Tutorial, page 16). Leaving one colour of pasta intact (this will be your base dough), cut the other into strips according to your design. You can use a knife, a pastry cutter, or simply a machine attachment.

2 Lay a sheet of your base dough out flat and give it a light spritz. For stripes, carefully lay the cut pieces parallel with the long edge of the bottom sheet. For squiggles, go wild. Just note that you will achieve a cleaner pattern by minimising overlaps and keeping the strips as flat and unkinked as possible.

3 Roll back through the machine on one setting thicker than that used to initially sheet the dough, or stepping through to your desired thickness. Cut and shape as required.

DOUBLE-SIDED STRIPES 

1 Select two or more egg doughs of different colours and work each into sheets slightly thicker than your final desired pasta thickness (see Basic pasta dough: Tutorial, page 16). Cut all into long strips according to your design.

2 On lightly floured baking paper, arrange the strips side-by-side, lightly wetting the inner edges with a brush or your finger. They should form a sheet no wider than your pasta machine. Lightly flour the top side, roll gently with a rolling pin, roll back through the machine on one setting thinner than that used to initially sheet the dough, or stepping through to your desired thickness. Cut and shape as required.

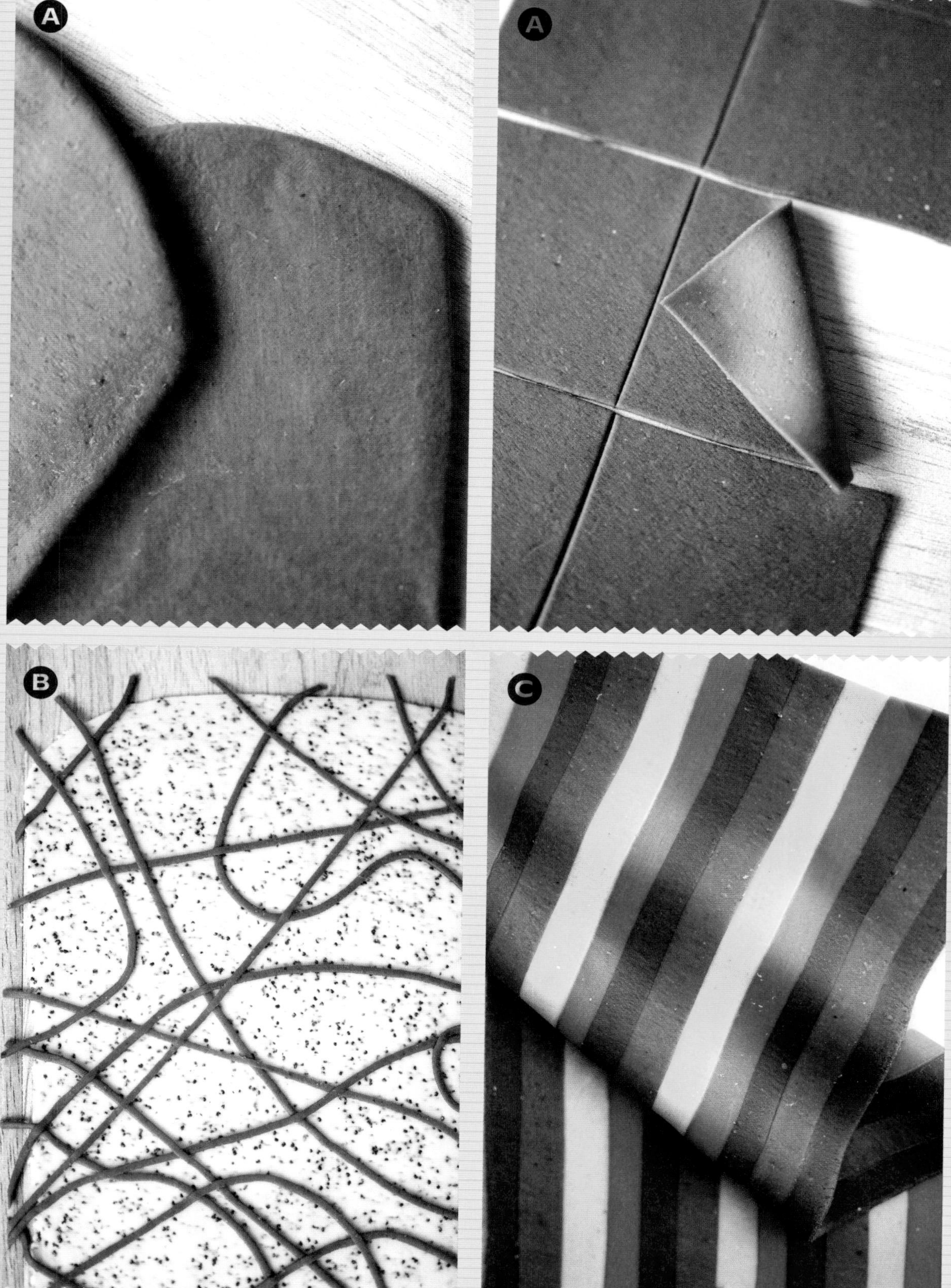
A
A
B
C

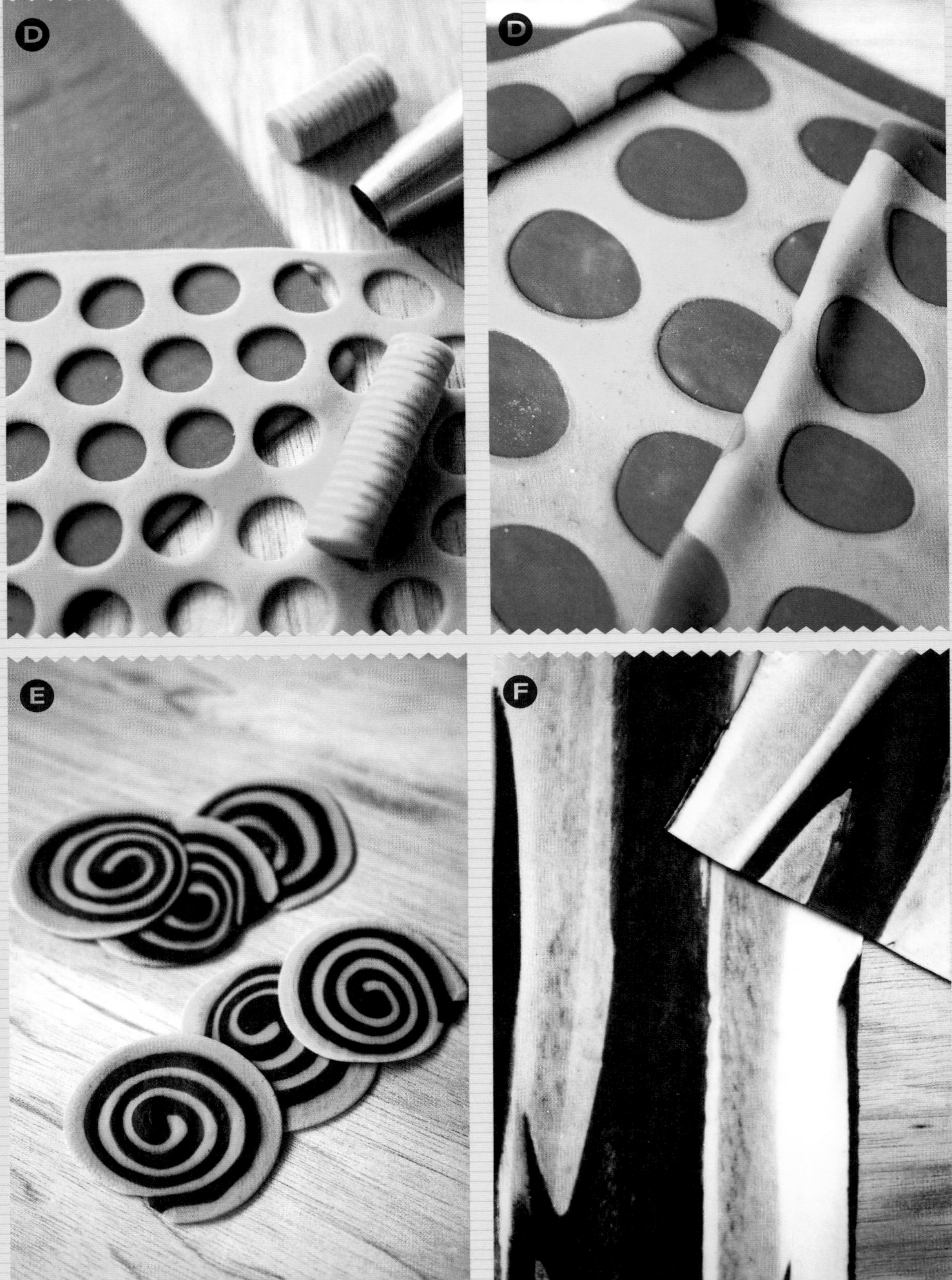
D
D
E
F

SPOTS (D)

1 Select two egg doughs of different colours and work each into sheets slightly thinner than your final desired pasta thickness (see Basic pasta dough: Tutorial, page 16).

2 Use a small round cutter, the end of a piping tip, or really any sharp round cutty thing and stamp holes into all sheets of one of the coloured doughs.

3 You know the drill: lay the one with the holes over the one without, with a little spritz in between. Roll back through the machine on one setting thicker than that used to initially sheet the dough. Note that if you decide to roll thinner, those spots will stretch.

SPIRALS (E)

1 Laminate two thick sheets of coloured pasta together (see Two-tone pasta, page 50) to a final thickness of about double the typical thickness for pasta. Roll the final sheet into a log the length of the shortest edge. For more colours or spirals, simply stack more sheets. Use a sharp knife to cut the dough log into rounds of 3–4 mm (⅛–¼ in) thickness.

2 If you're using each round for an individual piece of pasta, then simply roll them one at a time through the machine, working from the thickest setting that will grip the dough to your desired final thickness.

3 If creating a spiral sheet, use a single flat sheet of pasta as a base, and then arrange the spirals on top, squishing together to avoid too many gaps. Roll it back through the machine, starting at the thickest setting and working incrementally through to the pasta's final thickness.

MARBLING (F)

1 I'm not going to pretend that marbling (for us) is much more than cramming a whole heap of colours together and stuffing it through a machine to see what happens. There are, of course, more scientific ways of approaching pasta marbling, so we'll meet you halfway.

2 Select two or more colours of dough, and roll them out by hand into shortish, thick ropes. Intertwine, and then smoosh into a size and shape that looks vaguely like you could get it into the pasta machine.

3 Get it into the pasta machine, and then step through the settings to reach your desired pasta thickness. Note that you can fold and re-roll it through a couple of times to soften the effect, but repeat too many times and you'll end up with a solid-colour average of everything that you started with.

Rye and spinach fettuccine alla chitarra puttanesca

SERVES 4 | TOTAL TIME 45 MINS

At the heart of our family cooking, and indeed that of so many Italian families, is the concept of arrangiarsi. It's the beautiful notion of getting by, making do, overcoming obstacles, or making something from nothing. A philosophy of life that you can cook by. Our family also carried and passed on a cuisine built on cucina povera: 'the poor kitchen' or peasant cooking. Combined with arrangiarsi, the food that I remember from my earliest days was simple but stubbornly inventive: minimalist, but richer for it.

Puttanesca, famously named for either the creators of the dish or indeed a reputed pungency of their trade, takes simple improvisation's most likely ingredients and immortalises them in a recipe. As with so much great Italian cooking, this dish is born of haste and necessity, but nonetheless eaten with a joyful smack of the lips.

- ½ × quantity Whole egg and egg yolk dough (page 19), replacing durum semolina flour with rye flour
- ½ × quantity Spinach dough (page 24)
- 8 anchovy fillets
- 16 garlic cloves, peeled and lightly crushed
- 40 g (1½ oz) capers
- 120 ml (4 fl oz) extra-virgin olive oil
- 1 tablespoon dried red chilli flakes
- 800 g (1 lb 12 oz) tinned chopped tomatoes
- 180 g (6½ oz) black olives, pitted and sliced
- pinch of sugar
- salt and freshly cracked black pepper, to taste

Prepare sheets with both doughs, laminate back-to-back rolling to a final thickness of 1–2 mm (1/16–1/8 in) (see Multi-coloured pasta: Tutorial, page 50) and then cut into pasta using the widest setting on the chitarra (see Handmade pasta: Tutorial, page 33).

Lightly fry the anchovy fillets, garlic and capers in the oil for 3–4 minutes over a low–medium heat, or until the anchovies have broken down, the garlic is beginning to brown and the capers are slightly crispy. Add the chilli flakes and cook for a further 30 seconds, or until aromatic.

Add the tomatoes, black olives and sugar. Raise the heat to medium and cook for 10–15 minutes until the sauce thickens and the tomatoes lose their raw taste. Season with salt and pepper to taste.

Cook the pasta in lightly salted boiling water for 4–6 minutes until no raw white dough is visible when the pasta is cut into, and then drain, retaining half a cup of pasta water.

Toss the pasta into the sauce in the frying pan, adding pasta water if required to aid emulsification. Serve with a crack of black pepper.

ON PASTA

Though often still referred to as spaghetti alla chitarra, the wider settings on modern chitarre produce a pasta closer to fettuccine in dimensions. As such, useful substitutions are regular fettuccine or the more traditional spaghetti.

ON INGREDIENTS

By its nature, this is a dish that celebrates improvisation. If you have a few odds and ends that need using, this is the meal for it. Just don't go too wild. Or do, but don't mention my name if serving to Napoletani.

Two-tone tomato linguine amatriciana

SERVES 4 | TOTAL TIME 55 MINS

Tomatoes have always been at the centre of my food world, and are characteristic of southern Italian cooking. They share a tenacity with those hardy southerners too. Long after Tomato Day has passed, enough passata stashed away to last us until next summer, little tomato plants will inevitably spring up between the pavers or through the grass. Perhaps I'm just not thorough enough when hosing down my concrete.

We grew up with them fresh, dried out in the sun by Nonna's careful hand, bubbled slowly for hours, or indeed tipped out of a tin in a hurry. This recipe celebrates the latter, with a classic sauce stripped of even onion and garlic, and a pasta that doubles down on the glorious tomato by including paste in the dough itself.

- 1 × quantity Tomato dough (page 24)
- ½ × quantity Whole egg dough (page 18)
- 150 g (5½ oz) guanciale, cut into matchsticks
- 2 tablespoons extra-virgin olive oil
- 400 g (14 oz) tinned whole tomatoes
- sugar, to taste
- 60 g (2 oz) pecorino Romano, finely grated, plus extra to serve
- salt and freshly cracked black pepper, to taste

Prepare sheets of each dough and then combine into two-tone laminated sheets (see Multi-coloured pasta: Tutorial, page 50), rolling to a thickness of about 1 mm (1⁄16 in). Cut into linguine (see Handmade pasta: Tutorial, page 33).

Fry the guanciale with the olive oil in a pan over a medium heat for 4–5 minutes until crispy. Add the tomatoes, breaking up with a wooden spoon, and season to taste with a pinch or two of sugar. Lower the heat to low–medium and cook for 20–25 minutes, stirring occasionally.

Boil the pasta in a large pot of salted water for 6–8 minutes, testing for doneness, and drain lightly, retaining a cup of pasta water. Transfer to a mixing bowl and stir the cheese into the hot pasta until evenly coated (pour a little pasta water in if too dry), then add it all to the sauce in the frying pan.

Stir well, season to taste, and serve with extra cheese and a crack of black pepper.

ON PASTA

Bucatini (see page 82) is a fantastic and more traditional pairing for amatriciana, but a sauce of such simplicity will pair well with just about anything.

ON INGREDIENTS

I also love to cook this with a little diced onion, added in right after the guanciale, and gently cooked for 10–15 minutes before proceeding with the tomatoes.

TUTORIAL

Busiate

Busiate resembles and is sometimes referred to as fusilli, though it is made by hand rather than extruded. It's also typically a pasta of only flour and water, but we sometimes use an egg dough for a bit of variety.

Note that this tutorial carries on from the long and multi-coloured pasta tutorials, preceding a pair of two-tone busiate recipes. As such, we'll begin with a method utilising fettuccine-like strands of pasta, before demonstrating the more traditional process. You'll recognise the latter as a natural complement to the Pici, gemelli, lorighittas: Tutorial (page 66).

1 Prepare strands of egg dough fettuccine pasta (see page 18) to a thickness of about 1 mm (1⁄16 in) (see Handmade pasta: Tutorial, page 33), then roll around a thick wooden skewer or narrow dowel at an angle of about 45 degrees. Slide the pasta off.

2 Note that when using flat pasta like this to make busiate, it may hold its shape better if left on the skewer for a few minutes to dry. To avoid slowing yourself down, keep a handful of skewers at the ready.

1 The more traditional preparation of this pasta uses only flour and water. Roll your rested dough out into long thin sausages of around 5 mm (¼ in) in width. Chop into 15–20 cm (6–8 in) lengths.

2 With a length lying at 90 degrees to yourself, wrap the furthest end of it around the tip of a skewer lying offset at 45 degrees.

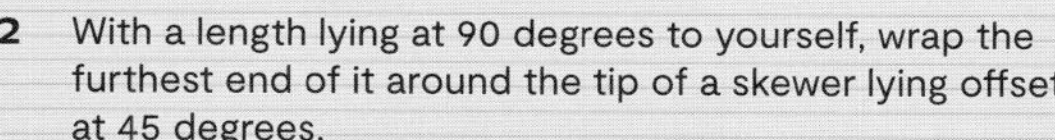

3 Roll the skewer towards you, allowing the dough to wrap around it. Slide off carefully.

NOTE For both of these methods, if the final shape sticks to the skewer, a slight and gentle roll back in the opposite direction will help to unstick it. Allow the pasta to air-dry for a couple of hours to better hold its shape when cooked.

Tri-colour busiate with butter and cheese

SERVES 6 | TOTAL TIME 45 MINS

I can't write a pasta book without including one of my childhood's greatest culinary pleasures: tri-colour packet pasta, with butter melted directly into the bowl, served under a mound of freshly grated cheese.

We lived a long way from school and work, and some nights there just wasn't time to prepare much else for dinner. Or at least that's what we told ourselves. I'd scramble around the backyard collecting kindling in the dying light, as the pasta water boiled, and then quickly warm my hands by the fire to the familiar sound of bowls hitting the table.

There's something oddly comforting about a simple, fast dish at the end of a long day. So, while you should probably have a few greens on the side, embrace a simple bit of butter and cheese every now and then.

- ½ × quantity Whole egg dough (page 18)
- ½ × quantity Spinach dough (page 24)
- ½ × quantity Paprika dough (page 21)
- 60 g (2 oz/¼ cup) butter
- 60 g (2 oz) pecorino Romano, grated
- salt and freshly cracked black pepper, to taste

Roll all three doughs out into sheets of about 1 mm (1⁄16 in) thickness and cut into fettuccine (see Handmade pasta: Tutorial, page 33), then roll into busiate (see Busiate: Tutorial, page 58). Cook in a large pot of salted water for 4–5 minutes. Test for doneness, then drain, leaving the pasta slightly wet.

While the pasta is still hot, melt in the butter and the cheese, stirring well.

Season to taste with salt and serve with a crack of black pepper on top.

ON PASTA

Halving doughs can be tricky when you're talking odd numbers of eggs and yolks. To halve the spinach dough in this recipe, use 2 eggs, and be prepared to add a little flour if it's too sticky. Of course, any other dough will also take its place just fine: beetroot (beet) (see page 21), spirulina (see page 20) and turmeric is one (earthier) alternative grouping. Add turmeric in the same ratio as you would spirulina.

ON INGREDIENTS

Well. I mean, it's butter and cheese. Nothing further to add here. Use salted or unsalted butter – just season accordingly.

Wild olive busiate with fried anchovy and tomato

SERVES 4 | TOTAL TIME 55 MINS

Two of the clearest and most joyful memories that I have of my first visit to Italy when I was four are of me loudly pretending that I was being kidnapped as my dad tried to load me into the car across from the Colosseum, and sitting in the back seat of a cousin's car as we hurtled through acres of olive trees in my nonna's hometown of Melicuccà. I'd grown up on olive oil, and loved it from a young age, so I was fascinated staring out of the window at those endless sloping fields of sagging nets, loaded with olives.

We still consume shocking amounts of olive oil to this day. I shudder to recall the time that we ran out and had to buy it from the top shelf of the supermarket, where it comes in ridiculous little bottles, less than 4 litres (135 fl oz/16 cups) at a time. Anyway, despite the amount of pasta that we cook with olive oil, it only recently occurred to me that I should try working the olives themselves into the dough.

The first time that we tried it, cut as pappardelle, my wife and I did that mute bewildered rage thing where you suddenly become very Italian and flap your hand around like you're using a tiny whisk, sideways. This handmade busiate takes that same delicious dough and rolls it into sauce-catching spirals, paired with a simple, classic sauce.

- 1 × quantity Wild olive dough (page 24)
- 6 garlic cloves, sliced
- 80 ml (2½ fl oz/⅓ cup) extra-virgin olive oil
- 8 preserved anchovy fillets
- 400 g (14 oz) vine-ripened cherry tomatoes, quartered lengthwise
- freshly cracked black pepper, to serve

Either sheet the pasta to a thickness of 1 mm (1/16 in) and cut into fettuccine (see Handmade pasta: Tutorial, page 33), or roll out into long, thin sausages of about 5 mm (¼ in) in diameter. Form into busiate (see Busiate: Tutorial, page 58).

Gently sauté the garlic with the olive oil in a frying pan over a medium heat for 3–4 minutes until aromatic and only just beginning to brown. Add the anchovies and fry for a further 1–2 minutes, stirring.

Add the tomatoes and allow to soften for 5 minutes before squashing with a wooden spoon. Lower the heat and cook for another 15 minutes, adding a little water if the sauce becomes too dry.

Cook the busiate in a large pot of salted water for 4–5 minutes before testing for doneness; drain, retaining a little pasta water. Stir into the sauce, adding some pasta water if necessary to aid emulsification.

Serve with cracked black pepper.

ON PASTA

A sauce like this goes with just about anything. Try longer pasta like fettuccine (see page 34) and spaghetti (see page 34) with smoother tomatoes, short and tube pasta like fusilli and rigatoni (see page 118) with chunkier.

ON INGREDIENTS

If you find anchovies too fishy, try adding a few splashes of garum in their place for a more subtle umami flavour. If you just can't get enough, use both.

On embracing the present

Making pasta, amongst all else, has become a sort of family meditation. Sitting down to that particular home-cooked meal that we've made together, every weekend, lends a semblance of control to a life of otherwise borderline chaos. Aldo's week is exclusively relative to Pasta Day; his calendar year counted off by them. I couldn't tell you the number of Sundays that I've eased into a chair with a huge bowl of pasta and a relieved sigh.

Having a constant like that, woven into what we eat and share, also keeps us grounded in the present. We buy fresh ingredients in the morning, prepare them in the afternoon, and eat together at night. As we sit down at the table, we're all inevitably grappling with our own turmoils and triumphs, reflecting on days of sickness and sadness spent slumped over our pasta, or those of celebration and clinking glasses. It means that when times are hard, this little ritual is a physical reminder that it will pass; when they're good, we're reminded to treasure them.

So, is it hard to make pasta with two small children, especially on those tougher days? It certainly doesn't make it any easier, but at the same time it wouldn't be the same without them. Don't get me wrong, they rarely stick around for the entire thing, but we plan for that. I keep small discrete processes for Aldo to drop by and participate in, or I set aside enough dough for him to quickly make into one serve of pasta. So far, Elio has a selection of wooden tools to chew on, and dough scraps to try and stuff in his mouth when I'm not looking. Aldo, in particular, is always present and involved in an integral way if he feels like it, but the show can go on if his toddler agenda has a last-minute scheduling clash.

I don't write this to suggest that you need children in the kitchen, or even children in general, but just to highlight that thirty seconds turning the pasta handle can give anyone a little ownership over the food that they're about to eat. Don't underestimate the capacity for children to pick up skills in the kitchen, or the value and empowerment that they'll get from it.

The same goes for those cooking without children, or alone. Pasta doesn't continue to impress because it's difficult, but because someone's hands have toiled to create it from flour and water. So, if nothing else, do yourself a favour and make some pasta.

LEFT Aldo making pasta out the back in Canberra

'When times are hard, this little ritual is a physical reminder that it will pass; when they're good, we're reminded to treasure them.'

TOP LEFT Elio checking the pasta

TOP MIDDLE Aldo putting on the coffee

TOP RIGHT Rachel and the boys

BELOW Nonna/Ma making pasta with us in Perth

Pici, gemelli, lorighittas

These three shapes are included here together, as their forms largely follow on from one another. All are traditionally made with only flour and water (see pages 22–23).

TO MAKE PICI Ⓐ

1 Form the dough into a thick log, then stretch it out into long thin ropes of around 3–5 mm (⅛–¼ in) in diameter. Do this by rolling it backwards and forwards, gradually moving your hands outwards from the middle; cut into smaller pieces as you work should the length become too cumbersome. If the dough is too slippery, spritz it very lightly to help it grip the bench and your hands. Cut into lengths of 25–30 cm (10–12 in).

2 Note that pici are commonly described as closer to 1 cm (½ in) in diameter, but I personally find this too thick. By the time the centre is cooked, the outside is a long way over. Or you get so sick of waiting for them to cook that you give up and eat them half-done. A 3–5 mm (⅛–¼ in) diameter will still give you that irresistible al dente centre with a soft surface.

FOR GEMELLI Ⓑ

1 Begin with similar ropes of dough to the pici, though closer to 3 mm (⅛ in) in diameter. Fold each rope in half, pressing the ends together, then anchor one end under one hand as you roll the opposite end away from yourself. The two halves should twist together as you roll. Chop into 5–6 cm (2–2½ in) pieces. Note that a more traditional method is to roll them to size, as opposed to cutting longer pieces into smaller.

LORIGHITTAS Ⓒ

1 Lorighittas are also formed from the same straight ropes of dough as the pici; we prefer a thickness of about 3 mm (⅛ in). Wrap the rope around your middle three fingers twice, and then pinch the ends together to close the double loop. Break off any excess rope, saving it for the next piece. Take one loop and weave it through the other until you are left with a single intertwined loop.

Pici with potato and beans

SERVES 4 | TOTAL TIME 1 HR 20 MINS

This is one of Nonna's classics, a comforting and simplistically delicious dish known as pasta vaianera, from the old Calabrese word for 'green beans'. The smell and taste of these humble ingredients together is one that takes me straight back to Nonna's little linoleum kitchen.

As with so many classics, it's one that can be thrown together in a hurry and cooked with little fuss. If we ever unexpectedly found ourselves at Nonna's around mealtime, she'd say 'non ci'mporta, ci arranciamu', 'it's no problem, we'll manage', and then produce a dish just like this. Often with fresh ingredients from her garden, sometimes sausage dried in the garage or fresh from a jar of lard, and various preserved bits and pieces made from seconds that her regular visitors would drop off or trade.

It was just how they did things: that whole generation that transplanted into their little pockets of Australia a self-sustainability originally born of necessity. But when I really think back, I do remember the sly smile of pride that Nonna would allow herself as we gawked at her huge basil leaves, bigger and greener than anyone else's, or pulled together a last-minute meal seemingly out of thin air. And of course. There are few things as satisfying as a simple meal made honestly, with ingredients you've grown, shared with people you love.

- 1 × quantity Strong flour dough (page 23)
- 2–3 garlic cloves, chopped
- 100 ml (3½ fl oz) extra-virgin olive oil
- 600 g (1 lb 5 oz) roma (plum) tomatoes, chopped
- 600 g (1 lb 5 oz) potatoes, cut into quarters or eighths
- 300 g (10½ oz) green beans, trimmed
- 300 g (10½ oz) zucchini (courgette), chopped into thick batons
- 1 small handful of basil leaves
- salt and freshly cracked black pepper, to taste

Prepare the pici using the strong flour dough and roll relatively thinly, about 3 mm (⅛ in) (see Pici, gemelli, lorighittas: Tutorial, page 66).

Gently sauté the garlic in the olive oil in a saucepan for 5–10 minutes over a low heat until soft but not browning; stir consistently. Add the tomatoes and raise the heat to medium.

Stir in the potatoes, beans, zucchini and basil with 200 ml (7 fl oz) water. Cover and cook for around 45 minutes until the potato has softened slightly and the sauce has thickened. Leave uncovered on the heat for a few minutes if the sauce is too runny. Season to taste.

Boil the pici in a large pot of salted water until cooked, around 4–6 minutes. They should be firm to the bite, but with no raw white dough visible in the middle. Note that thicker pici can take significantly longer to cook. Drain, retaining a little pasta water.

Toss the cooked pasta directly into the sauce and stir, adding a little pasta water if required.

ON PASTA

Nonna always served this with long pasta, usually spaghetti or similar, which works well alongside the long pieces of vegetables. That said, you could always dice everything finer to combine with shorter pasta.

ON INGREDIENTS

There are numerous ways that you could prepare this, incrementally adding the vegetables into a pot of water, separately cooking the potatoes. Nonna would have pulled her 'perché?' face at anything more complicated than dropping it all into the pot together. Sometimes the simplest method makes for the most honest-tasting food.

Sumac pici cacio e pepe

SERVES 4 | TOTAL TIME 35 MINS

Just about every pasta that you can imagine benefits from a mountain of grated cheese and a crack of black pepper. Though photographically underrepresented in this book, due to the limitations set by needing to actually see the dish, we typically mound on enough finely grated cheese to comprehensively obscure whatever's underneath. Turns out that the Romans felt much the same way about the whole thing, and so gifted the world cacio e pepe: a plate of cheese and pepper, with a little pasta stirred in.

As far as I'm concerned, this is a dish straight from the heart. There's nowhere to hide and everything to bare. I seek it out in restaurants to see whether they really care about their craft and customers, and I make it for those I know to be appreciative of simple things crafted beautifully. So, if you love someone, make them cacio e pepe; and if you want them to love you back, make it with pecorino.

- 1 × quantity Strong flour dough (page 23), made with 2 tablespoons sumac (see page 22)
- 60 ml (2 fl oz/¼ cup) extra-virgin olive oil
- 2 teaspoons freshly cracked black pepper, plus extra to serve
- 300 g (10½ oz) pecorino Romano, very finely grated, plus extra to serve

Form the pici using the strong flour dough to a thickness of 3–5 mm (⅛–¼ in) (see Pici, gemelli, lorighittas: Tutorial, page 66). Cook in a large pot of salted water for 4–6 minutes, testing for doneness. Retain a cup of pasta water.

Warm the oil in a large frying pan over a low heat. Add the cracked pepper and stir for around 30 seconds, until fragrant.

Drop the pasta directly from the pot into the frying pan and stir vigorously to create an emulsion from the oil and water. Stir in the cheese, adding pasta water as required to create a creamy sauce. You may need to use quite a lot.

Serve with grated cheese and cracked pepper. Of course.

ON PASTA

You guessed it: this one's normally served with spaghetti. There's really no need to limit yourself to tradition though, just learn from it, so try any long pasta as a decent substitution. Bucatini (see page 82) and spaghetti alla chitarra (see page 34) would be my picks.

Pici is a great option because it has the same flour and water simplicity of extruded spaghetti, but can be made by hand, taking on a beautiful rustic form.

ON INGREDIENTS

Don't be afraid to go hard on the cheese and pasta water.

Gemelli with slow-cooked pork shoulder ragù

SERVES 8 | TOTAL TIME 5 HRS 15 MINS

A sure-fire way to a satisfying meal is simple ingredients cooked for a long time. And meat. I remember a couple of decades back, the last giant family party that we had. The kind that has so many 'uncles' and 'cousins' that you're reminded of the fact they're actually placeholder titles used to avoid convoluted explanations of exactly whose cousin's great-uncle-in-law you're talking to. The type where even the less familiar hair gel and gold chain side of the family turns up. And the type with a whole lamb roasting on a giant spit, manned by an assortment of portly bristled men holding beers and shouting at each other over the smoke in beautifully broken English and Calabrian.

Family events have been whittled down now by time and distance, and it's been many years since I had room for a spit in the backyard, so our slow-cooked meals these days all happen at a scale that can fit into a casserole pot. This is one of our go-tos, served with simple, bitey gemelli.

- 1 × quantity Semolina dough (page 22)
- 1.2 kg (2 lb 10 oz) pork shoulder, trimmed of fat and cut into large chunks
- salt and freshly cracked black pepper, to season
- 80 ml (2½ fl oz/⅓ cup) extra-virgin olive oil
- 1 fennel bulb, sliced
- 3–4 wild boar bocconcini sausages, diced or sliced (alternatively, use 250 g/9 oz other salami)
- 1 carrot, finely diced
- 1 onion, finely diced
- ½ garlic bulb, minced
- 1 tablespoon fresh thyme leaves
- 1 rosemary sprig
- ½ teaspoon dried chilli flakes
- 400 g (14 oz) tinned crushed tomatoes
- 800 ml (27 fl oz) passata (puréed tomatoes)
- 1 teaspoon sugar
- pinch of salt
- 250 ml (8½ fl oz/1 cup) red wine
- 2 bay leaves
- 1 teaspoon fennel seeds, dry roasted and coarsely ground
- 1 tablespoon black pepper, coarsely ground
- pinch of ground cayenne pepper

Preheat the oven to 160°C (320°F). Hand-roll the pasta dough into ropes of around 5 mm (¼ in) in thickness and then form into gemelli (see Pici, gemelli, lorighittas: Tutorial, page 66).

Season the pork and brown in a hot, lightly oiled flameproof casserole. If you don't have one, you can use a large frying pan, later transferring to an ovenproof dish. Remove the meat and deglaze with a splash of water. Set the liquid aside. Turn the heat down to low.

Add the olive oil, fennel, sausage, carrot, onion, garlic, thyme, rosemary and chilli flakes and gently fry until the onion is translucent. Expect this to take 20–30 minutes, stirring continuously. Add the browned pork back in and mix through the soffritto before pouring in the crushed tomatoes, passata and deglazing liquid. Season with the sugar and a pinch of salt. Swill 800 ml (27 fl oz) of water around in the empty can and passata bottle to collect any leftovers and add to the pot. Then mix in the wine, bay leaves, fennel seeds, black pepper and cayenne. Season and give it a good stir.

Bring to the boil, cover, and transfer to the oven. If using a frying pan to this point, transfer the ragù to an ovenproof dish or pot first. Cook for 4–5 hours, stirring occasionally, and check the moisture levels regularly. Add water if necessary to prevent it becoming too dry. Remove from the oven and stir gently to break up the chunks of meat until it is at a satisfactory consistency to serve.

Cook the gemelli for 8–10 minutes in a large pot of salted water; test for doneness and then drain, retaining a cup of pasta water. Stir into the sauce, adding a little water back in to assist emulsification.

ON PASTA

This ragù is well-suited to most pasta shapes; it's really just a matter of what you feel like eating. We also love this with rigatoni (see page 118), or stuffed into paccheri (see page 118).

ON INGREDIENTS

This recipe also works well with beef, or a mix of beef and pork. Likewise, try playing around with the salami. We rarely cook this one the same way twice, often varying it based on what looks good at the butcher and deli counter, or what we've unearthed at the bottom of the freezer.

Saffron lorighittas with blue swimmer crab

SERVES 4 | TOTAL TIME 55 MINS

As soon as I was old enough, I learned how to dive. I was so young that I had to rope my dad into doing the course with me, which we both actually loved. At least, up until my Rescue Diver training where I had to drag him out of the ocean and up the beach draped across my shoulders. Or when he suddenly accelerated in front of me in a tight limestone swim-through off Rottnest Island, kicking loose my mask and regulator and leaving me in a maelstrom of blood, sand and confusion. Or that other time that he went navigator on a deep dive, only to overshoot the wreck with such speed that by the time I caught him sitting on the sand at 32 metres we had only enough air left to decompress and surface.

I digress. One of our favourite after-school activities was night diving in the river. Admittedly, there wasn't a whole heap to see, but it was fun skimming over the sand by compass-bearing and torchlight. We'd usually charge around in the middle of the river like that for a while before heading to the nets around the baths, where we'd settle in to spot seahorses. Out there with us on the sand were blue swimmer crabs, or blue mannas as they were known back home, and we'd regularly startle each other by appearing suddenly face-to-face out of the gloom as we all dashed about our business.

In the landlocked world of my early adult life I came to rely on dishes like this for the light and breezy nostalgia they evoked; of days and sunsets passed by the sea. I'm finally back on the coast now, with my own band of beach-lovers, and I can confirm that it also goes well with the sound of waves breaking. I haven't yet gotten the old man back into a wetsuit, but I'm working on it.

- 1 × quantity Semolina dough (page 22), made with 1 teaspoon pre-soaked saffron (see page 22)
- 2 tablespoons fine sea salt
- 4 raw blue swimmer crabs
- 2 tablespoons extra-virgin olive oil
- 20 g (¾ oz) butter
- 1 teaspoon dried red chilli flakes
- 2 garlic cloves, minced
- 2 tablespoons verjuice
- 2 tablespoons lemon juice
- 2 tablespoons lemon zest
- 1 small handful of flat-leaf (Italian) parsley, finely chopped
- 4 finger limes, flesh only, to serve
- sea salt flakes and pepper, to taste

Hand-roll the dough into long ropes of 3–5 mm (⅛–¼ in) and prepare lorighittas (see Pici, gemelli, lorighittas: Tutorial, page 66).

Fill a large stockpot with water, add the salt and bring to the boil. Drop the crabs in and boil for 6–8 minutes. They should turn orange and float when ready. Transfer to a bowl of iced water and leave for 20 minutes. Once cool, crack open and remove the flesh.

Heat the oil and butter in a frying pan over a low–medium heat, then gently fry the chilli and garlic for 3–4 minutes.

Add the verjuice and lemon juice with the crab meat and stir. Allow to reduce slightly before mixing in the lemon zest and parsley.

Drop the pasta into a large pot of boiling, lightly salted water and cook until firm but done, around 8–10 minutes. Drain, retaining a cup of the pasta water, and then add the pasta to the frying pan. Turn the heat up to high and use a little pasta water to assist emulsification with the sauce as you toss it together.

Serve with finger lime, a sprinkle of salt flakes and a crack of black pepper.

ON PASTA

We enjoy this dish just as well with long pasta, especially linguine or tagliolini (see page 34).

ON INGREDIENTS

Finger limes are like a citrusy caviar, adding a delicious Aussie lift to this dish. There are endless varieties, all with unique flavours that you can pair fresh with just about anything. Of course, they're not an essential ingredient to this dish, but I highly recommend trying them if you ever get the chance.

Fileja

The most rustic pasta in our repertoire, fileja warms the heart with its unassuming presence and joyfully irregular shape.

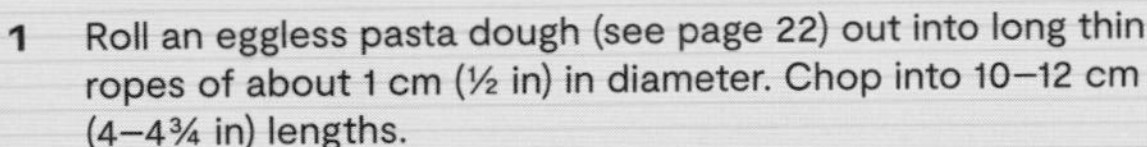

1 Roll an eggless pasta dough (see page 22) out into long thin ropes of about 1 cm (½ in) in diameter. Chop into 10–12 cm (4–4¾ in) lengths.

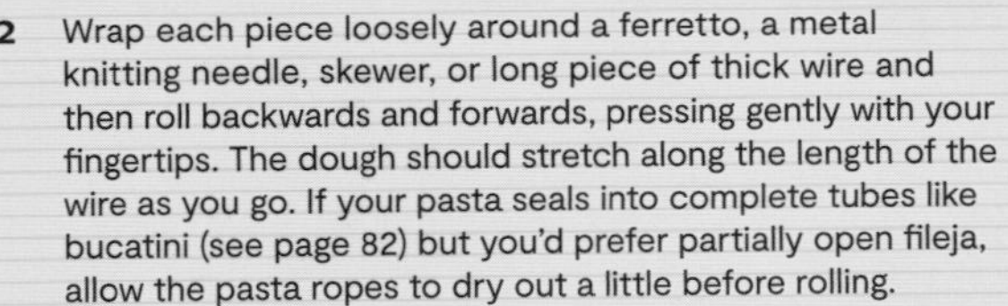

2 Wrap each piece loosely around a ferretto, a metal knitting needle, skewer, or long piece of thick wire and then roll backwards and forwards, pressing gently with your fingertips. The dough should stretch along the length of the wire as you go. If your pasta seals into complete tubes like bucatini (see page 82) but you'd prefer partially open fileja, allow the pasta ropes to dry out a little before rolling.

NOTE On the rolling implement: in times of emergency, I may have taken wire cutters to coat hangers.

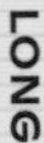

Fileja with avocado and lemon

SERVES 4 | TOTAL TIME 40 MINS

I've always struggled to pick a favourite pasta, but fileja would be up there. There's just something special about its rough unpredictability, appropriately Calabrian. You make it still with care, but it's a loose, coarse kind of care that celebrates imperfection and pairs perfectly with a simple sauce.

Now, Nonna, for the long days she'd spend preparing a family meal, ate quite modestly herself. There was a noble pride in frugality amongst that generation of Italian migrants. I remember her friends and brothers constantly travelling across town in pursuit of wholesale fruit and veggie bargains, buying up large amounts and then redistributing amongst multiple households, including Nonna's. Often derided by outsiders of her time, I'm sure that Nonna would now nod and harrumph approvingly to know that concepts of cucina povera, self-sustainability, and uncomplicated food are finally having their day.

One of her favourite quick meals, decadent by today's standards but born as a cheap and efficient use for something you just had too much of, was pasta with avocado.

- 1 × quantity Semolina dough (page 22)
- ½ onion, diced
- 2 tablespoons extra-virgin olive oil
- 4 avocados
- juice of 1 lemon, plus extra to serve
- salt and freshly cracked black pepper, to taste

Use your fresh semolina dough to form long 5 mm (¼ in) thick ropes, then cut and form into fileja (see Fileja: Tutorial, page 76).

Gently fry the onion in the olive oil over a low–medium heat for 15 minutes until transparent. As that's cooking, blend together the avocado and lemon juice to your desired consistency and season to taste.

Boil the pasta in a large pot of salted water until cooked but still firm, around 5–6 minutes. Mix the avocado in with the onions in the frying pan, then use tongs to transfer the fileja to the sauce. Stir well, adding a little pasta water as necessary for a smooth, even coating.

Serve with cracked black pepper and an extra squeeze of lemon juice.

ON PASTA

This sauce would work with pretty much anything, but for a substitution close to fileja, try bucatini (see page 82), busiate (see page 58), or fettuccine (see page 34).

ON INGREDIENTS

This is also a dish that works well with an uncooked sauce; just lose the onions and oil.

Cracked pepper fileja with onion and pecorino

SERVES 4 | TOTAL TIME 55 MINS

Pasta with onions is a Calabrian dish, traditionally made with the famous Tropea onion: a beautiful purple variety with less acid than other onions and, as a result, a characteristic sweetness that shines through. As well as less tears over the chopping board. This dish uses regular brown onion though, quite deliberately.

Aside from the ubiquitous prickly pear designating most southern Italian-Australian households, many Italian migrants brought (smuggled) in quite a narrow selection of fruit and vegetables, highly specific to their old homes and specialties. These became the notoriously meticulous gardens from which many meals drew their primary ingredients. For whatever reason, the Tropea onion just didn't catch the boat with our little familial network. Instead, Nonna adapted and made do with whatever she could find to fill her ingredient gaps, and I grew up with a taste for good old brown onions.

- 4 garlic cloves, smashed
- 2 tablespoons extra-virgin olive oil
- 600 g (1 lb 5 oz) onions, sliced
- 100 ml (3½ fl oz) white wine
- 1 × quantity Semolina dough (page 22), made with 1 tablespoon freshly cracked black pepper (see page 20)
- 100 g (3½ oz) pecorino Romano, grated
- 1 small handful of parsley, finely chopped
- salt and freshly cracked black pepper, to taste

Gently sauté the garlic in the olive oil in a large frying pan over a medium heat for 4–5 minutes. Add the onion, stir, and then deglaze with the wine. Allow around half of the wine to evaporate, then drop the heat to low.

Cook, stirring, for 30 minutes, adding a little water if it becomes too dry or begins to catch. The onion should turn a semi-translucent, deep brown. Remove the pan from the heat.

Roll the pasta dough into ropes of about 5 mm (¼ in) in thickness, then form into fileja (see Fileja: Tutorial, page 76).

Boil the pasta in a large pot of salted water for 5–6 minutes until no raw dough is visible when the pasta is cut into. Drop it directly into the onions, retaining a cup of pasta water.

Add the cheese and parsley, seasoning with salt and pepper to taste, then stir well. Use a little pasta water to aid emulsification.

Serve with cracked black pepper.

ON PASTA

Remember that cooking times will blow out substantially if you begin these rope-based shapes with thicker lengths of pasta. Always check your pasta before wildly flinging it from the stove.

We often mix cracked black pepper into whole egg dough, cutting it into fettuccine (see page 34), and that would work well here too.

ON INGREDIENTS

For a true taste of Calabria, try getting your hands on Tropea onions. They have less acid for their sugars to hide behind, so exhibit a unique sweetness.

Extruded pasta

Extruded pasta is a slightly different beast to other pasta dough. The concepts of moisture and gluten remain the same, but are applied differently. Our Extruded dough (page 25) is a little unconventional in that it contains egg, however it works well with a range of home-extruder options.

1 To prepare the dough, whisk the egg into the water and then gradually stir it through the plain (all-purpose) flour, semolina and salt. Mix it together using your fingers for about 10 minutes before refrigerating for half an hour. Note that the dough should look and feel a bit like buttered breadcrumbs, but hold together when pinched between your fingers. Add a small amount of water if it's too dry.

2 Set your extruder to its top speed and feed in loosely clumped balls of dough, around the size of walnuts. Avoid overfilling, and note that it may take a few minutes of the dough being kneaded inside the extruder before it begins to come out.

3 Chop the pasta using an extruder cutter or sharp knife as it reaches your desired length.

Spaghetti with burrata and breadcrumbs

SERVES 4 | TOTAL TIME 45 MINS

Though extruded pasta doesn't feature too often on Pasta Sundays, it's actually one of the first that Al and El each helped make. The crumbly, clumpy dough is perfect for small grabby hands, and once the machine's running it's a simple drop and chop job. Of course, I also couldn't write a pasta book without featuring the most quintessential of pasta, so here's an easy little spaghetti recipe to whip up with all hands, big and small.

- 1 × quantity Extruded dough (page 25)
- 60 ml (2 fl oz/¼ cup) extra-virgin olive oil
- 80 g (2¾ oz) dry breadcrumbs
- 50 g (1¾ oz) hot Calabrese salami, thinly sliced
- 1 garlic bulb, smashed, with skin removed
- 1 teaspoon dried red chilli flakes
- 100 g (3½ oz/2 cups) baby spinach leaves
- juice of ½ lemon
- 4 balls of fresh burrata
- 1 large handful of shelled pistachios, roughly chopped
- salt and freshly cracked black pepper, to taste

Use the extruded pasta dough to make spaghetti (see Extruded pasta: Tutorial, page 82).

Heat the oil in a frying pan over a medium–high heat, then brown the breadcrumbs. This should only take 10–15 seconds. Transfer to paper towel using a slotted spoon.

In the same pan, fry the salami as whole slices. Remove once they're crispy but before they turn brown, around 20–30 seconds. Add to the paper towel to drain.

Lower the heat to medium and gently fry the garlic and chilli flakes, stirring regularly. Once the garlic begins to brown, about 5 minutes, add the greens and allow to wilt for 2–3 minutes.

Cook the pasta for 6–8 minutes, test for doneness and drain, retaining some of the pasta water. Add the pasta to the frying pan and stir well, pouring back in a little water to assist emulsification, and stirring in the lemon juice.

To serve, form a mound of pasta on each plate and place a fresh burrata on top. Crumble the salami and sprinkle it over the pasta, along with the breadcrumbs, pistachios and a fresh crack of pepper.

ON PASTA

Alternatively, try this one with spaghetti alla chitarra or linguine (see page 34).

ON INGREDIENTS

Most things improve when you pop a burrata on top, but make sure that you buy them fresh. Some pasta dishes just aren't meant to be if the ingredients can't be of the highest quality, and this is truer still of simpler dishes like this one.

Squid ink bucatini con le sarde

SERVES 4 | TOTAL TIME 45 MINS

Though perhaps a little late in life, and unhelpfully complicated by its realities, if I could choose someone to be when I grow up, without a doubt I'd be Inspector Montalbano. Aside from refreshingly relatable traits, such as his warranted, weary grouchiness and exaggerated hand gestures, Montalbano is a man who pays food the respect that it deserves. Andrea Camilleri's novels, and closely adapted television series, feature a veritable dreamscape of food, and aren't shy of lengthy pauses in crime-fighting for the sake of a fragrant sun-drenched meal. Even if we can't all find a few hours in the middle of our work day to enjoy lunch by the sea or at home prepared by our housekeeper, relish your food like Montalbano and you'll live a life of true contentment.

Pasta con le sarde (pasta with sardines) is one of the great commissario's favourite dishes. You can find it in *Il cane di terracotta (The terracotta dog)*, when Adelina cooks it to celebrate Livia going home. Honestly, Livia, what a pest. It's a magnificently simple and fresh Sicilian dish, and the next best thing to an ocean swim and an espresso before a day spent fighting crime.

- 1 × quantity Extruded dough (page 25), made with 1 teaspoon squid ink (see page 24)
- 320 g (11½ oz) fennel, chopped, fronds reserved
- ½ onion, chopped
- 3 large anchovies
- 80 ml (2½ fl oz/⅓ cup) extra-virgin olive oil
- 50 ml (1¾ fl oz) white wine
- pinch of saffron threads
- 20 g (¾ oz) pine nuts
- 20 g (¾ oz) raisins
- 260 g (9 oz) fresh sardines, sliced into strips
- zest and juice of ½ lemon
- 25 g (1 oz) toasted breadcrumbs, to serve
- freshly cracked black pepper, to serve

Prepare the bucatini using the extruded squid ink dough (see Extruded pasta: Tutorial, page 82).

Gently fry the fennel, onion and anchovies in the olive oil over a medium heat until soft; 15–20 minutes. Add the wine and saffron, allowing it to reduce until almost dry. Stir in the pine nuts and raisins, then add the sardines, frying them until cooked – around 1 minute.

Cook the pasta by boiling it in a large pot of lightly salted water for 6–8 minutes. It's ready once no raw, white dough is visible when the pasta is cut into. Lightly drain, then drop directly into the pan with the sauce. Add the lemon zest and juice, and toss well. Serve with the breadcrumbs, fennel fronds and a crack of pepper.

ON PASTA

Plain bucatini would work just fine if squid ink's not for you, as would spaghetti (see page 34). Finely rolled pici (see page 66) would also make for a pleasant, though slightly heartier, pairing.

ON INGREDIENTS

Despite its bold seafood components, this is not an overly fishy dish if your sardines are nice and fresh. Stick to short cooking times and you'll have an overall light and subtle dish.

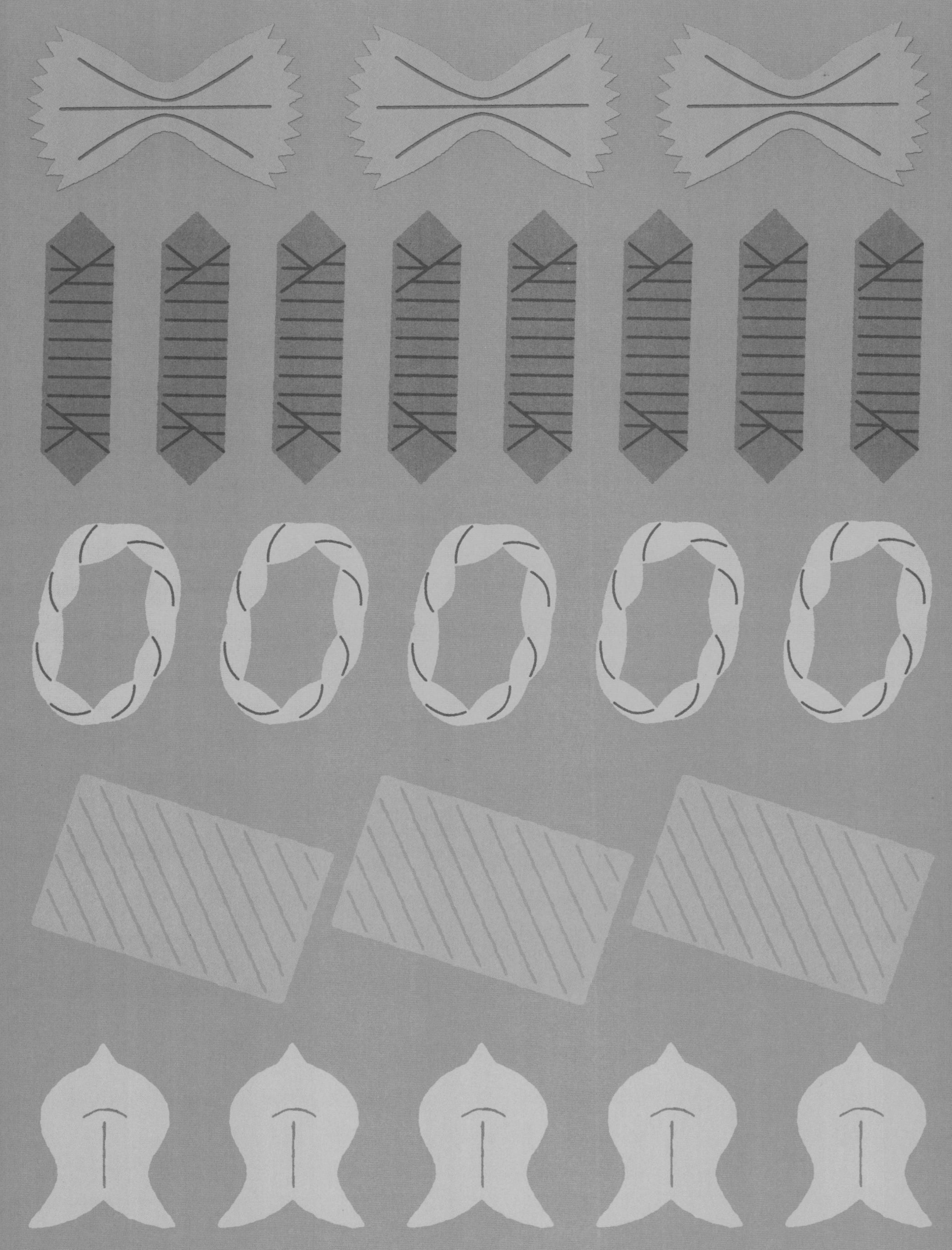

SHORT

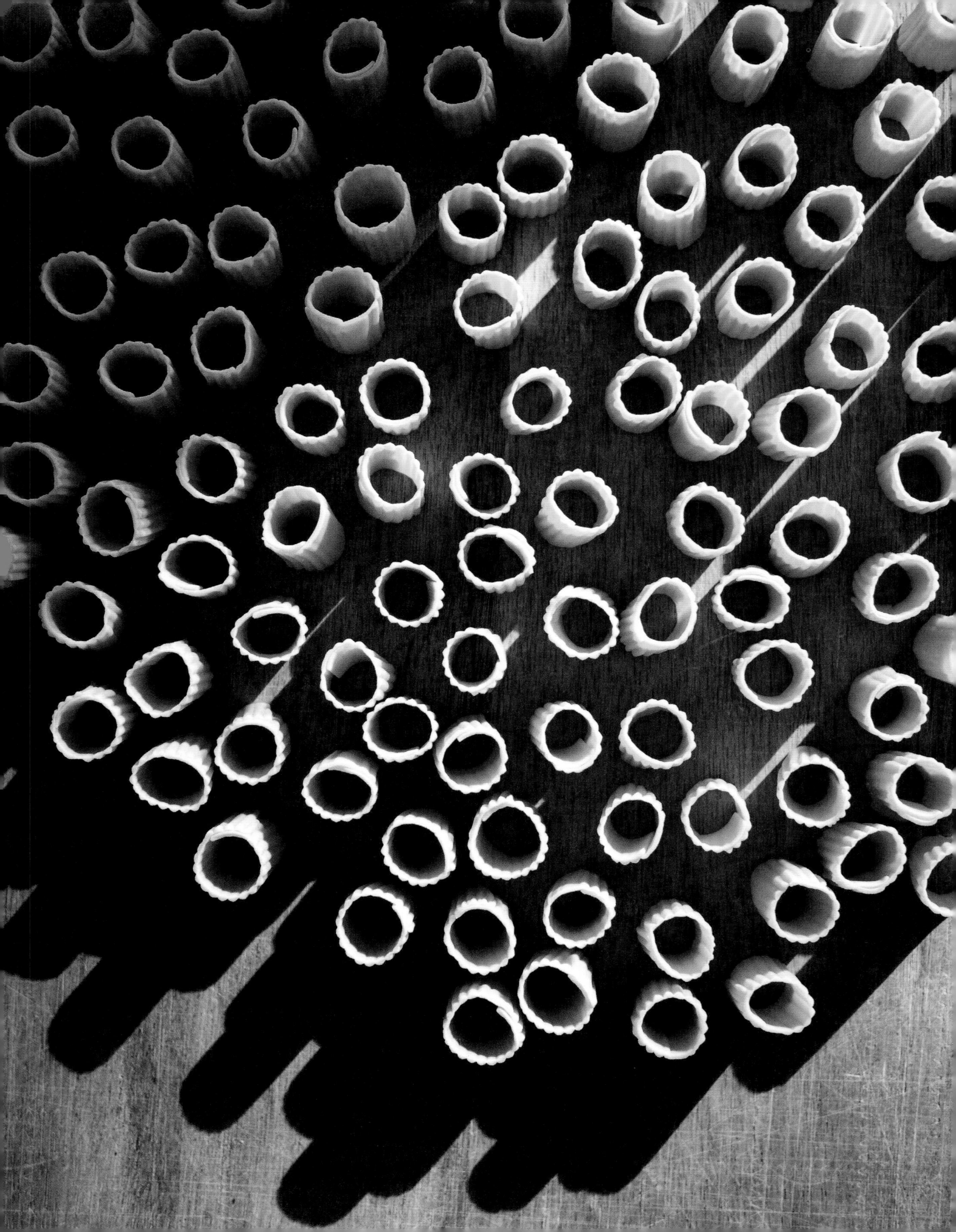

With shorter pasta, you begin to cross over into more involved shapes; designs that uniquely capture sauce and explore texture. This chapter covers our favourites: garganelli, sorpresine, farfalle, funghetti, and handmade tube pasta. As a kid, these were the kinds of shapes found exclusively in coveted packet pasta. Some, like rigatoni, are more traditionally left to extrusion. Others, like farfalle and funghetti, have simply been bought as dried pasta for so long that you rarely see them made fresh. Either way, they're rewarding shapes to try out in your own kitchen. Though it may be slow going at first, you'll quickly develop your own techniques and shortcuts, and discover a little meditation in the process.

Garganelli

Formed as they're rolled, garganelli truly bring an element of meditation to pasta-making. A wonderful handmade alternative to penne or rigatoni.

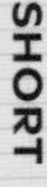

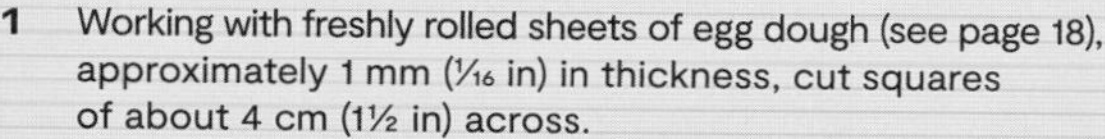

1 Working with freshly rolled sheets of egg dough (see page 18), approximately 1 mm (1⁄16 in) in thickness, cut squares of about 4 cm (1½ in) across.

2 Wrap each around a piece of 1 cm (½ in) diameter dowel, offset into a diamond alignment, and overlap the two opposing corners.

3 Then roll towards you across your pettine or gnocchi board, pressing down gently as you go. This will seal the pasta into a tube while forming its ridges. Gently slide off the dowel.

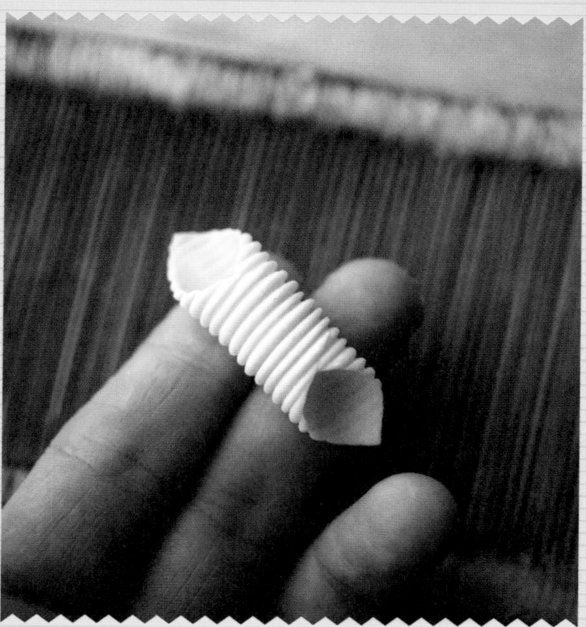

NOTE For an even less fiddly option, simply lie each square diagonally on the pettine with the dowel across the top. Tuck one corner over the dowel and roll up.

I find that larger garganelli will flatten out a little under their own weight. If you'd like to avoid this, just let them air-dry for a few minutes before rolling them 90 degrees and giving them a gentle poke in the side.

Garganelli with white sauce and chilli

SERVES 4 | TOTAL TIME 45 MINS

Obviously, with a name like mine, I am not 100 per cent Italian. Apart from a little curl to my hair, both naming rights and genes were claimed by my dad's half of the family. Needless to say, Grandma's table was very different to Nonna's. Her specialties included English classics like potato pie, toad-in-the-hole, pasties, and the crowd favourite amongst the Italian in-laws, a boozy trifle. At some point though, she introduced a little pasta herself, in the form of small foil pouches, readied with a few minutes in the microwave. I am unashamed to say that I was immediately addicted to instant pasta Alfredo.

Since old Alfredo first, rather theatrically, tapped into that faultless combination of cheese and butter, the sauce has been reinterpreted with milk, cream and even eggs. The variety that I encountered as a kid, rehydrated with some sort of chive-flavoured milk powder, was actually closer to a white sauce, and so that's the flavour that I go for when I feel like revisiting those sacrilegious TV dinners of my childhood. Now with a hint of chilli.

- 1 × quantity Whole egg and egg yolk dough (page 19)
- 50 g (1¾ oz) butter
- 40 g (1½ oz) plain (all-purpose) flour
- 500 ml (17 fl oz/2 cups) full-cream (whole) milk
- 60 g (2 oz) Parmigiano Reggiano, finely grated
- 1 teaspoon dried chilli flakes
- salt and freshly cracked black pepper, to taste

Make garganelli (see Garganelli: Tutorial, page 92), working with sheets of around 1 mm (1⁄16 in) thickness. Boil in a large pot of salted water for 4–5 minutes, test for doneness and then drain, retaining a cup of pasta water.

Melt the butter in a saucepan over a medium–high heat until it begins to foam, then stir in the flour and cook for 2 minutes, ensuring that it doesn't catch.

Gradually pour in the milk, whisking vigorously, and cook for a further 5 minutes until thickened. Remove from the heat and stir in the cheese and chilli.

Add the pasta into the sauce, pouring in a little pasta water as you stir (just enough to make the sauce smooth and not too dry, without it becoming too runny).

Serve with a crack of black pepper on top.

ON PASTA

Long pasta is a more typical pairing for a simple white sauce like this, so try tagliolini (see page 34), spaghetti alla chitarra (see page 34), or fettuccine (see page 34). Other tube pasta like macaroni and rigatoni (see page 118) will also do an excellent job of holding sauce.

ON INGREDIENTS

If you really want that Aussie packet pasta magic, leave out the chilli and add 1 tablespoon finely snipped chives.

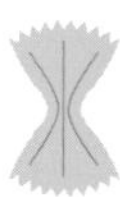

Garganelli with lamb, spinach and preserved lemon

SERVES 4 | TOTAL TIME 1 HR

Garganelli is a particularly pleasing pasta to make: like some sort of rustic penne, sealed as it's rolled. Al and I use a variety of surfaces to form those pleasing ridges, but our favourite is the traditional pettine (pasta comb), handcrafted from the old combs of textile looms. The resulting texture is well-suited to all sauces, but it's hard to deny my Southern roots and a preference for all things tomatoey.

This recipe swaps out our family's typical meat choice of pork and veal mince for lamb, and skips over the soffritto for a quick and easy sauce, full of punchy flavour.

- 1 × quantity Whole egg dough (page 18)
- 60 ml (2 fl oz/¼ cup) extra-virgin olive oil
- 2 garlic cloves, minced
- 400 g (14 oz) minced (ground) lamb
- 200 ml (7 fl oz) red wine
- 400 ml (13½ fl oz) passata (puréed tomatoes)
- 2 teaspoons dried oregano
- salt and freshly cracked black pepper, to taste
- 240 g (8½ oz) baby spinach leaves, loosely chopped
- 1 small preserved lemon, rind only, finely chopped
- 1 tablespoon crumbled feta

Roll out your fresh pasta dough into sheets around 1 mm (1⁄16 in) thick, and form into garganelli (see Garganelli: Tutorial, page 92).

Heat the oil in a large frying pan over a medium heat. Add the garlic and lamb, stir, and cook for 10–15 minutes until the lamb begins to brown and crisp up. Deglaze with the red wine and allow it to cook off, around 10 minutes.

Pour in the passata with the oregano, season to taste, and cook for a further 15–20 minutes.

Add the spinach and allow to wilt, about 5–6 minutes.

Cook the garganelli in a large pot of salted water for 4–5 minutes, or until done; drain, and stir directly into the sauce.

Serve with the preserved lemon and crumbled feta.

ON PASTA

We quite enjoy this with penne (rigate, obviously), or a longer pasta like fettuccine alla chitarra (see page 34).

ON INGREDIENTS

You can, of course, use store-bought preserved lemon. Alternatively, a fresh grating of lemon zest and a squeeze of lemon juice will do in a pinch.

Sorpresine

Meaning 'little surprises', sorpresine are probably the most delightful impostors of filled pasta, and a very cute way to use up unfilled pasta squares.

1 Cut fresh sheets of egg dough (see page 18) 0.8–1 mm (1⁄16 in) thick into squares of around 3–4 cm (1¼–1½ in).

2 Bring two opposite corners together to meet, gently pinching at their very tips to seal together into an open triangle.

3 Place a finger just inside each of the two openings, slightly below the corners, and bring the sides together. As you do this, a vertical crease will form behind the joined tip. Press your fingertips together firmly to join the dough together.

4 For smaller squares, or clumsier hands, try using your pinkie fingers to bring the pasta together. Or teeny tiny toddler fingers.

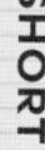

Cocoa-striped sorpresine with butter and balsamic

SERVES 4 | TOTAL TIME 45 MINS

Sorpresine is a truly delightful shape of pasta, and one that shines when served with an uncomplicated sauce. Plain butter preparations like this are also the perfect opportunity to introduce a little flair; the cocoa dough that stripes our sorpresine does add a unique and subtle depth of flavour, but is there just as much to please the eyes. Take this as an opportunity to have a little creative pasta fun in the kitchen, and then reward yourself with an easy finish.

1 × quantity Whole egg dough (page 18)

¼ × quantity Whole egg dough (page 18), made with 20 g (¾ oz) dark cocoa powder (in place of 20 g/¾ oz plain/all-purpose flour; see page 20)

60 g (2 oz/¼ cup) butter

salt and freshly cracked black pepper, to taste

splash of balsamic vinegar, to serve

Roll out both doughs into sheets of 0.8–1 mm (1⁄16 in) thickness. Cut the cocoa dough into tagliolini, then combine into sheets of squiggly striped pasta (see Multi-coloured pasta: Tutorial, page 50). Form into sorpresine (see Sorpresine: Tutorial, page 98).

Cook the pasta in a large pot of salted water for 3–4 minutes, or until firm but no longer raw, and then drain, retaining one cup of pasta water.

Melt the butter in a large frying pan over a low heat and pour in a generous glug of pasta water. Stir vigorously to emulsify, and season to taste with salt.

Add the pasta directly to the pan, coating evenly with the sauce, and adding more pasta water if required.

Serve with a splash of balsamic vinegar and crack of black pepper.

ON PASTA

There's obviously no need to stripe your pasta, but if you do, a simple sauce like this will let you show it off. Substitute with really anything you can think of.

ON INGREDIENTS

Treat yourself to a fancy bottle of balsamic and elevate this sauce from a lazy afterthought to a considered, minimalist delight.

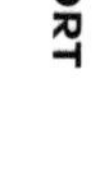

Mixed herb sorpresine in minestra

SERVES 4 | TOTAL TIME 1 HR 45 MINS

Minestra, across all associated interpretations and subcategories, is a big old bowl of undeniable comfort. More often than not, as the weather gets colder, there'll be some variation of this simmering away on the stove. In fact, as a kid, that familiar smell was a pretty accurate indicator of how chilly it would be getting overnight.

Amongst other reasons to love minestra is the fact that it's an easy one-pot meal. Dedicate a good amount of time to sweating out and developing that soffritto, and then it's just a staged dropping-in of everything else. For this recipe we've stuck the seasoning into the pasta itself, creating a rich and buttery dough, folded into a wonderfully grabby little shape.

- 1 × quantity Whole egg and egg yolk dough (page 19), made with 2 tablespoons finely chopped mixed herbs (see page 20)
- 60 ml (2 fl oz/¼ cup) extra-virgin olive oil
- 4 garlic cloves, finely chopped
- 1 onion, diced
- 1 carrot, diced
- 1 celery stalk, diced
- 200 g (7 oz/4 cups) baby spinach leaves
- 2 litres (68 fl oz/8 cups) chicken or vegetable stock
- 2 fresh rosemary sprigs
- 200 g (7 oz) fresh cherry tomatoes
- 400 g (14 oz) tinned white beans, drained and rinsed
- grated hard cheese, to serve
- salt and freshly cracked black pepper, to serve

Prepare pasta sheets of 0.8–1 mm (1/16 in) thickness, and form sorpresine (see Sorpresine: Tutorial, page 98).

Put the olive oil, garlic, onion, carrot and celery into a large cold pot. Set over a low–medium heat and cook for 25–30 minutes, stirring frequently. The vegetables should soften and the onions become slightly transparent without browning.

Stir in the spinach leaves, allowing them to wilt, before pouring in the stock with the rosemary and cherry tomatoes. Partially cover, raise the heat to medium, and cook for 30–40 minutes.

Add in the white beans and sorpresine, cooking until the pasta is ready, around 5–6 minutes.

Serve with grated cheese and cracked pepper.

ON PASTA

Any small pasta works well in minestra, and you can create a great dish with long, fine shapes too, but possibly our favourite substitute is maltagliati. Maltagliati literally means 'badly cut', and describes any and all offcuts from the pasta-making process. It's hard to beat the satisfaction of rough and irregular (and otherwise discarded) pieces of dough in a cosy soup.

ON INGREDIENTS

Bump up your veggie count with green beans, chicory, kale, or really whatever you've got in the garden or fridge. And for extra depth and a heartier profile, try adding pancetta or Italian sausage into your soffritto.

TUTORIAL

Farfalle

Delicate butterflies, formed with an elegant pinch in the centre.

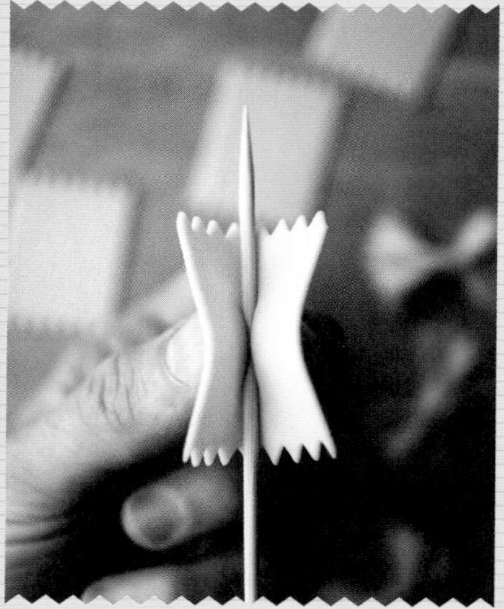

1 Begin with fresh egg dough pasta sheets (see page 18) of around 1 mm (1/16 in) thickness, cutting them into small rectangles of 2–3 × 4–5 cm (¾–1¼ × 1½–2 in). Traditionally, the shorter edge is cut with a zigzag. I should note that most dimensions in these tutorials are a combination of tradition and personal preference; absolutely do your own thing if you're feeling adventurous.

2 To form the pasta, make three pinches, similar to pleating, across the middle of each rectangle. The first pinch is from one side to about one-third of the way in, then the same on the other side, before squeezing those two pleats together firmly. Ensure that you keep a channel down the centre to allow water to flow in and cook the pasta evenly. These pinches are so important, that this shape is known as stricchetti in Emilia-Romagna, meaning 'pinch' in local dialect.

NOTE An alternative to hand-pinching the channel is to lay a thin skewer lengthwise down the centre of each rectangle. Pinch a little peak on either side of it, and then squeeze together over the top, pulling the skewer out to complete the shape.

Spelt farfalle alla Norma

SERVES 4 | TOTAL TIME 1 HR 5 MINS

There may be no better complement to eggplant (aubergine) than tomato. Or so I'm happy to claim, with my southern-Italian bias creeping in. This classic is a favourite around here, served with just about any pasta, and sometimes even reduced down and spread across a pizza. It's reminiscent of my ma's famed parmigiana, with pillowy, oil-rich eggplant, smooth tomato sauce, and punchy, salty cheese.

As hard as it is to go wrong with regular white pasta, we do enjoy the earthy variations and extra heartiness that often come with the introduction of a non-standard flour. This dish is one that I find benefits from a little something extra in the dough, marrying the flavour of the pasta even better to that of the sauce. But, of course, take this as an opportunity rather than a hard recommendation. Whatever you make with your own hands will be the best choice.

- 800 g (1 lb 12 oz) eggplant (aubergine), cubed
- 80 ml (2½ fl oz/⅓ cup) extra-virgin olive oil
- salt and freshly cracked black pepper, to taste
- 1 × quantity Whole egg and egg yolk dough (page 19), replacing the durum semolina flour with spelt flour (see page 20)
- ½ onion, diced
- 2 garlic cloves, minced
- 1 small handful of basil
- 700 ml (23½ fl oz) passata (puréed tomatoes)
- sugar, to taste
- ricotta salata, to serve

Preheat the oven to 220°C (430°F). Toss the eggplant in 2 tablespoons of the olive oil, seasoning with salt and pepper, then arrange in a single layer on a baking tray lined with baking paper. Roast for 20–30 minutes, or until the eggplant has shrunk and begun to brown; shuffle and toss occasionally.

While the eggplant roasts, roll your pasta dough into 1 mm (1⁄16 in) thick sheets and form into farfalle (see Farfalle: Tutorial, page 105).

Sauté the onion and garlic in the remaining olive oil, stirring in a large frying pan over a medium heat for around 10 minutes, or until softened and beginning to brown. Add the basil, crushing gently, and cook for a further 1–2 minutes, or until the leaves turn a bright green.

Pour in the passata and add a pinch of sugar if it tastes bitter; season with salt and pepper. Swill around a cup of water inside the passata bottle to collect any leftover tomato, and add to the pan. Cook over a low–medium heat for 15 minutes, stirring occasionally.

Stir in the cooked eggplant and cook for a further 10 minutes.

Boil the farfalle in a large pot of salted water until cooked, around 3–4 minutes, then scoop out directly into the sauce. Stir well and serve with grated ricotta salata on top.

ON PASTA

You'll most often find tube and long pasta prepared alla Norma, like rigatoni (see page 118) and spaghetti (see page 34), but it can be very moreish with smaller pasta too. Other substitutions with a little more bite include casarecce (see page 148) and gemelli (see page 66).

ON INGREDIENTS

In the distant past, I remember Ma leaving her sliced and salted eggplant (aubergine) to drain for a while before cooking to remove excess water and to offset its bitterness. As both a lazy adult and enthusiastic eater of eggplant, I'm going to say don't waste your energy. It seems that enough time has elapsed for eggplants to have had much of that bitterness bred out of them. I never salt, and have had no complaints. Avoid the usual warnings of bitterness, like big hard seeds, and you'll be right.

Beetroot polka-dot farfalle with parsley and anchovy

SERVES 4 | TOTAL TIME 25 MINS

Parsley and anchovy is another classic Calabrian pairing, as informed by a childhood spent scrutinising pizza slices for hints of fish, or the Russian roulette that was selecting a zeppola not bearing a stinky little anchovy in the centre.

I've obviously well and truly come around and, in fact, we've made sure that the boys have a taste for all foods fishy, pungent and pickled. Little Al's even onto the chilli now. These colourful butterflies are another balance of fancy pasta to simple sauce, the chlorella pairing nicely with the anchovy, and the polka-dots taking the minds of those not so convinced of the fish. In theory.

- ½ × quantity Whole egg dough (page 18), made with 1 tablespoon freeze-dried beetroot powder (see page 21)
- ½ × quantity Whole egg dough (page 18), made with ½ tablespoon chlorella (see page 20)
- 4 garlic cloves, chopped
- 80 ml (2½ fl oz/⅓ cup) extra-virgin olive oil
- 10 preserved anchovy fillets
- 1 teaspoon dried red chilli flakes
- 1 handful of parsley, finely chopped
- juice of ½ lemon
- salt and freshly cracked black pepper, to taste

Roll both doughs into sheets, stamping holes in the chlorella sheets and laminating onto the beetroot sheets (see Multi-coloured pasta: Tutorial, page 50). Roll to a final thickness of around 1 mm (1/16 in), then cut and form into farfalle (see Farfalle: Tutorial, page 105). Cook for 3–4 minutes, testing for doneness, and then drain. Retain a cup of pasta water.

Gently sauté the garlic in the olive oil in a large frying pan over a medium heat for 1–2 minutes, being sure not to let it brown. Add the anchovies and chilli, mashing the anchovies with a wooden spoon. Cook for a further 30 seconds.

Add the farfalle, parsley and lemon juice to the pan; stir well, seasoning to taste and pouring in a little pasta water if required. Serve.

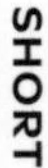

ON PASTA

Parsley and anchovy has to be one of the easiest and most versatile sauces that we serve our pasta with. It will pair beautifully with most short and long unfilled pasta.

ON INGREDIENTS

We grow and buy two main types of parsley: curly and flat-leaf (Italian). Nonna always used curly, and so that's what we've used here, but flat-leaf parsley (which looks a bit like coriander/cilantro) does have some extra pepper to it and is equally excellent.

On laughter

Nonna was famously unafraid of the rough foothills neighbourhood that she lived in. In fact, she thrived on being the most terrifying part of it, and had chosen for herself a life of low-level vigilantism, policing the streets and local public transport in an unwavering, hard-eyed Nonna manner that, frankly (and especially with the language and cultural barrier), must have seemed straight-up insane to anyone without Nonna experience. She was the hero that the Armadale railway line deserved, but not the hero that anyone in their right mind would have asked for.

Every time we sat down for a meal with her she'd have a new tale to tell, always very matter-of-factly: how she'd lectured another gang of teenagers loitering at the train station about why they should be in school, or how she'd stood over another litterer doggedly harassing them until they picked up their rubbish and put it in the bin. She'd tell punks to pull their pants up and take their piercings out, drunks to get themselves together, and loudmouths to be quiet. Even parents weren't safe from the Transperth Terror. She'd peer into prams and tell mothers off if their kids looked too dirty, and harangue them unrelentingly if they were smoking near their children. If anyone ever asked her for bus money after she'd laid into them about their unkempt appearance, she would mercilessly retort: 'povera sì, sporca perché?' 'Poor yes, but dirty, why?'

Even walking to the station, she was notorious for chastising neighbours over their untidy front yards. Though as my mum points out, she would provide positive feedback too, to the effect of 'it's good to see that you finally did something about that'.

The cousins all found it hilarious, although I remember our parents wringing their hands in expectation of this tiny, old, partially intelligible woman one day cornering the wrong reprobate. When we'd joke about it, Nonna would allow herself a wry smile: equal parts admission of how mad it all was, and quiet pride. It was particularly mad because I really don't think that our family virtue is strength, so much as stubbornness. We dig in our heels and either get our way or take everyone down in flames with us. I hear tales of my nonna's mum, who would dress like a man so that she could cart baskets of rocks on her head to rebuild bombed bridges back in Calabria, and I know that it's the same stubbornness that now locks me into unresolvable stand-offs with my three-year-old.

I digress. Laughter and food go hand in hand. While Nonna's local exploits often started us off, I remember so much merriment over the dinner table. I guess that laughter just comes more easily with good food in your belly. So, pasta ties me to happy times and wonderful people. Cooking for our families today, I think that all of us cousins still feel the warmth of moments that we unintentionally but irrevocably created for ourselves more than 30 years ago with little more than a funny story and a shared meal.

'I guess that laughter just comes more easily with good food in your belly.'

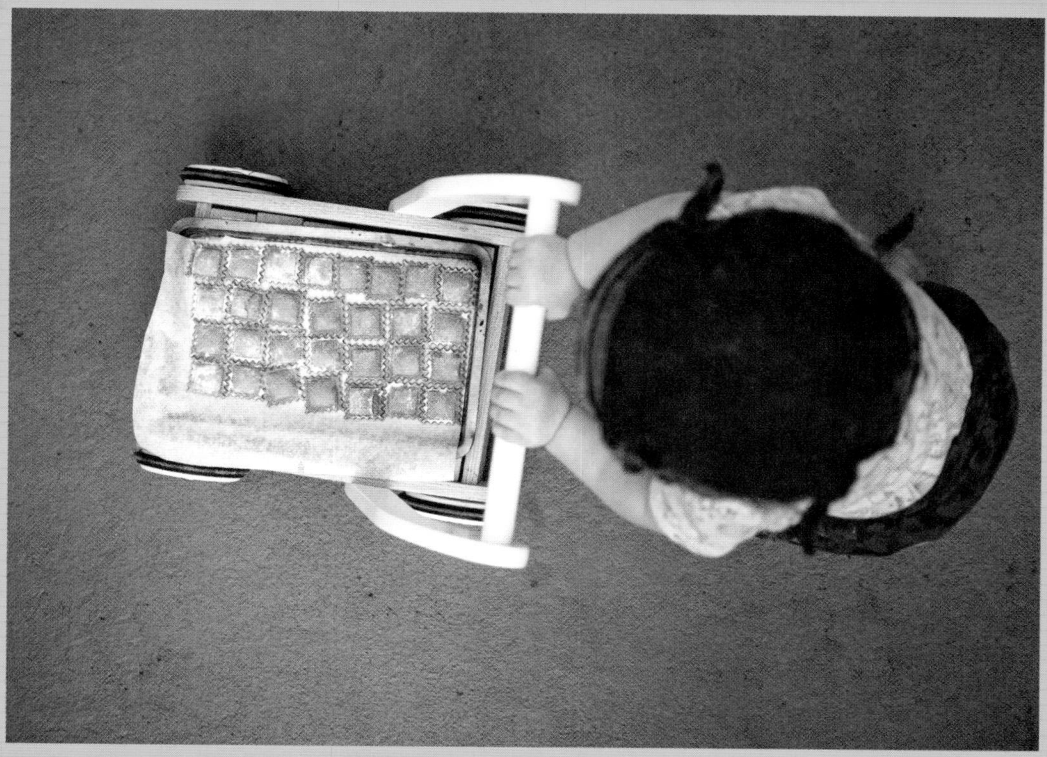

Aldo delivering pasta in Canberra. Newly walking, we'd have to turn him around whenever he hit a wall.

Making pasta together in Perth

Funghetti

One for just about any occasion, funghetti are hearty with a thick sauce, shapely in a thin sauce, and an all-round satisfying mouthful of pasta.

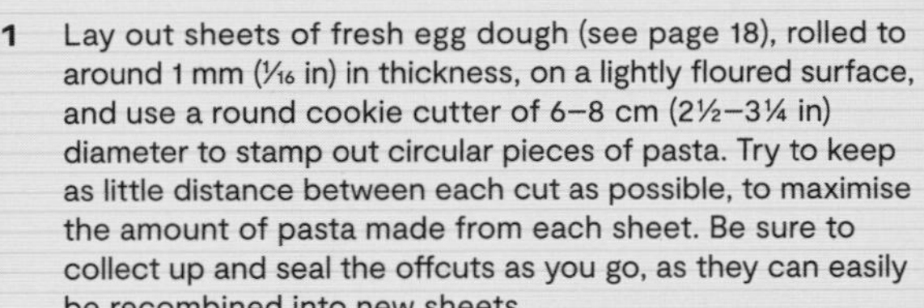

1 Lay out sheets of fresh egg dough (see page 18), rolled to around 1 mm (1⁄16 in) in thickness, on a lightly floured surface, and use a round cookie cutter of 6–8 cm (2½–3¼ in) diameter to stamp out circular pieces of pasta. Try to keep as little distance between each cut as possible, to maximise the amount of pasta made from each sheet. Be sure to collect up and seal the offcuts as you go, as they can easily be recombined into new sheets.

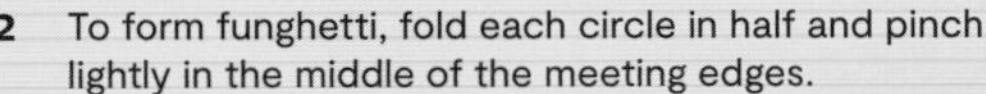

2 To form funghetti, fold each circle in half and pinch lightly in the middle of the meeting edges.

3 Fold it in half again by bringing the outer corners together. Gently pinch the inner walls (not the corners) together to complete.

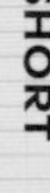

Dark rye funghetti with truffle, artichoke and cocoa crumb

SERVES 4 | TOTAL TIME 35 MINS

Funghetti is a shape that we introduced into our repertoire out of respect to my brother: a biologist who, in perhaps typical biologist manner, is a little obsessed with mushrooms. It also happens to be an excellent shape for playing around with multi-coloured dough and pairing with all manner of sauces.

This sauce, really a pesto, is a little reference to Nonna's jar of giardiniera: an eternal presence on the top shelf of her fridge. More specifically, it's to make up for the years that I spent carefully eating around the artichoke. Made with a little truffle oil, and served with smooth mascarpone and crunchy breadcrumbs, this dish is just about the most texture and flavour you can get without doing any real cooking.

- 2 slices sourdough bread, stale and crusty
- 1 tablespoon dark cocoa powder
- 50 g (1¾ oz) butter
- ½ × quantity Whole egg and egg yolk dough (page 19)
- ½ × quantity Whole egg and egg yolk dough (page 19), made with dark rye flour in place of durum semolina flour (see page 21)
- 320 g (11½ oz) artichoke hearts, preserved in brine
- 2 garlic cloves, minced
- 1 small handful of fresh parsley, coarsely chopped
- 1 small handful of fresh basil, coarsely chopped
- 4–5 mint leaves, coarsely chopped
- 80 g (2¾ oz) roasted walnuts
- 60 g (2 oz) Parmigiano Reggiano, grated
- 1 teaspoon white truffle olive oil
- 120 ml (4 fl oz) extra-virgin olive oil
- salt and freshly cracked black pepper, to taste
- fresh truffle, sliced, to garnish (optional)
- 80 g (2¾ oz) mascarpone

Blitz the sourdough and dark cocoa powder in a food processor until coarsely crumbed. Melt the butter in a frying pan over a medium–high heat and stir in the breadcrumbs. Cook for 1–2 minutes until crunchy. Remove to paper towel.

Form each dough into sheets (see Handmade pasta: Tutorial, page 33), and then laminate into two-tone pasta (see Multi-coloured pasta: Tutorial, page 50). Roll the pasta dough into 1 mm (1/16 in) thick sheets, and then cut into circles. Recombine the offcuts to produce new sheets and stamp more circles to minimise waste and maximise pasta. Form into funghetti (see Funghetti: Tutorial, page 112).

Cook the funghetti in boiling salted water for 4–5 minutes. Test for doneness, and then drain, retaining a cup of pasta water.

Combine the artichoke, garlic, parsley, basil, mint, 60 g (2 oz) of the walnuts, the Parmigiano, white truffle olive oil and olive oil in a mortar and pestle or food processor. Season to taste.

Toss the pesto with the pasta in a large mixing bowl, adding a little pasta water as required to produce a smooth sauce that evenly coats the funghetti. Serve with thin slices of truffle (if using), the cocoa breadcrumbs, dollops of mascarpone, the remaining walnuts and a crack of black pepper.

ON PASTA

As a pesto variation, this sauce works perfectly with any traditional pesto pasta. We especially love foglie d'ulivo (see page 154), fazzoletti, trofie and linguine (see page 34).

ON INGREDIENTS

This measure for artichokes is after draining. Gross weight will vary by brand, but generally expect a 560 g (1 lb 4 oz) jar to yield 320 g (11½ oz) of actual artichokes.

In the simplest terms, white truffle tends to have a stronger, more pungent flavour, while black is a little subtler and earthier. Both can be difficult and expensive to get hold of, particularly fresh, so adjust truffle oil and garnish components according to whatever you can find.

Paprika and cracked pepper funghetti arrabbiata

SERVES 4 | TOTAL TIME 55 MINS

We're going back to basics with the unbeatable arrabbiata. This well-known sauce is made with only the good stuff: garlic, chilli and tomato (and a few stray basil leaves). I heard someone comment once, after tasting their recently served penne all'arrabbiata, that it was 'just a tomato sauce with chilli in it'. Firstly, yes; secondly, the only time that's a bad thing is when it's done poorly. Or, as was the case on this occasion, served with that blight on the pasta world that is penne lisce. If you're a nonna, serve your enemies the evil eye; if you're a pasta-maker, penne lisce.

Anyway, the two-tone funghetti that little Al helped develop for this dish is flavoured with paprika and cracked pepper, to capture that fiery arrabbiata without overshadowing it. Cook it all up with enough chilli to redden the face, and pair it with a big, fruity red.

- ½ × quantity Whole egg dough (page 18), made with 3 teaspoons paprika (see page 21)
- ½ × quantity Whole egg dough (page 18), made with 2 teaspoons freshly cracked black pepper (see page 20)
- 5–6 garlic cloves, chopped
- 60 ml (2 fl oz/¼ cup) extra-virgin olive oil
- 2–4 teaspoons dried red chilli flakes, or to taste
- 1 small handful of basil leaves
- 800 g (1 lb 12 oz) crushed tomatoes
- sugar, salt and freshly cracked black pepper, to taste
- grated hard cheese, to serve

Form your two doughs into sheets (see Handmade pasta: Tutorial, page 33), and then laminate back-to-back (see Multi-coloured pasta: Tutorial, page 50). Roll sheets to a final thickness of 1–2 mm (1⁄16–⅛ in). Cut into circles and shape into funghetti (see Funghetti: Tutorial, page 112).

Fry the garlic in the olive oil in a large frying pan over a medium heat for 4–5 minutes, or until aromatic but still soft.

Add the chilli flakes and basil, frying for a further 30–60 seconds, then pour in the tomatoes. Season with a pinch of sugar if required, and some salt and pepper. Reduce the heat to low and cook for 20–25 minutes, stirring occasionally.

Boil the funghetti in a large pot of salted water for 4–5 minutes until done, then drain, retaining a cup of pasta water.

Stir the cooked pasta directly into the sauce, adding a little pasta water to help it combine.

Serve with grated hard cheese and a crack of black pepper.

ON PASTA

You'll often find this sauce paired with a more common pasta like penne or spaghetti, but there's no reason to limit yourself; this arrabbiata will go with just about anything.

There's no need to make this with a laminated dough as we have, although the paprika does add a little extra depth and the pepper even more spice.

ON INGREDIENTS

This is arrabbiata in its simplest form, but sometimes we add a little salami of some kind, making it more like a spicy amatriciana. And if you're wondering about those crispy basil leaves in the photo – simply fry them up before the garlic for 30 seconds, or until they turn bright green with oil spots beginning to appear.

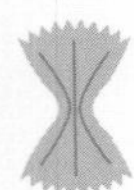

Tube pasta

Though typically extruded, most tube pasta can also be made by hand. This book contains recipes for rigatoni and the very closely related tortiglioni, but the same process can be used to make paccheri and cannelloni. Even macaroni, if you have the time and inclination. To form handmade bucatini, simply follow the steps in Fileja: Tutorial (page 76), but allow the dough to seal around and into itself instead of remaining open.

1. Begin with sheets of fresh egg pasta (see page 18); we roll them to about 2 mm (⅛ in) in thickness for our tube pasta.

2. For rigatoni, cut into rectangles of 4.5–5 × 7 cm (1¾–2 × 2¾ in); for tortiglioni we prefer closer to 6 × 7 cm (2½ × 2¾ in).

3. Wrap each piece around a thick piece of dowel, 1.4 cm (½ in) in diameter, overlapping the narrow edges parallel to each other. Run a finger gently along the join to press closed. If it's not sticking, brush a little water in between the overlap.

4. For rigatoni, lie the dowel and pasta parallel with the lines on a gnocchi board; for tortiglioni, offset diagonally. Press down gently and roll towards yourself until the pasta is evenly grooved. This roll will also reinforce the join.

NOTE The dimensions of the rectangle (or square) will depend on the diameter of your dowel, or vice versa. If you're not sure, use a piece of paper cut to size to figure it out before you start rolling your dough.

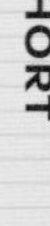

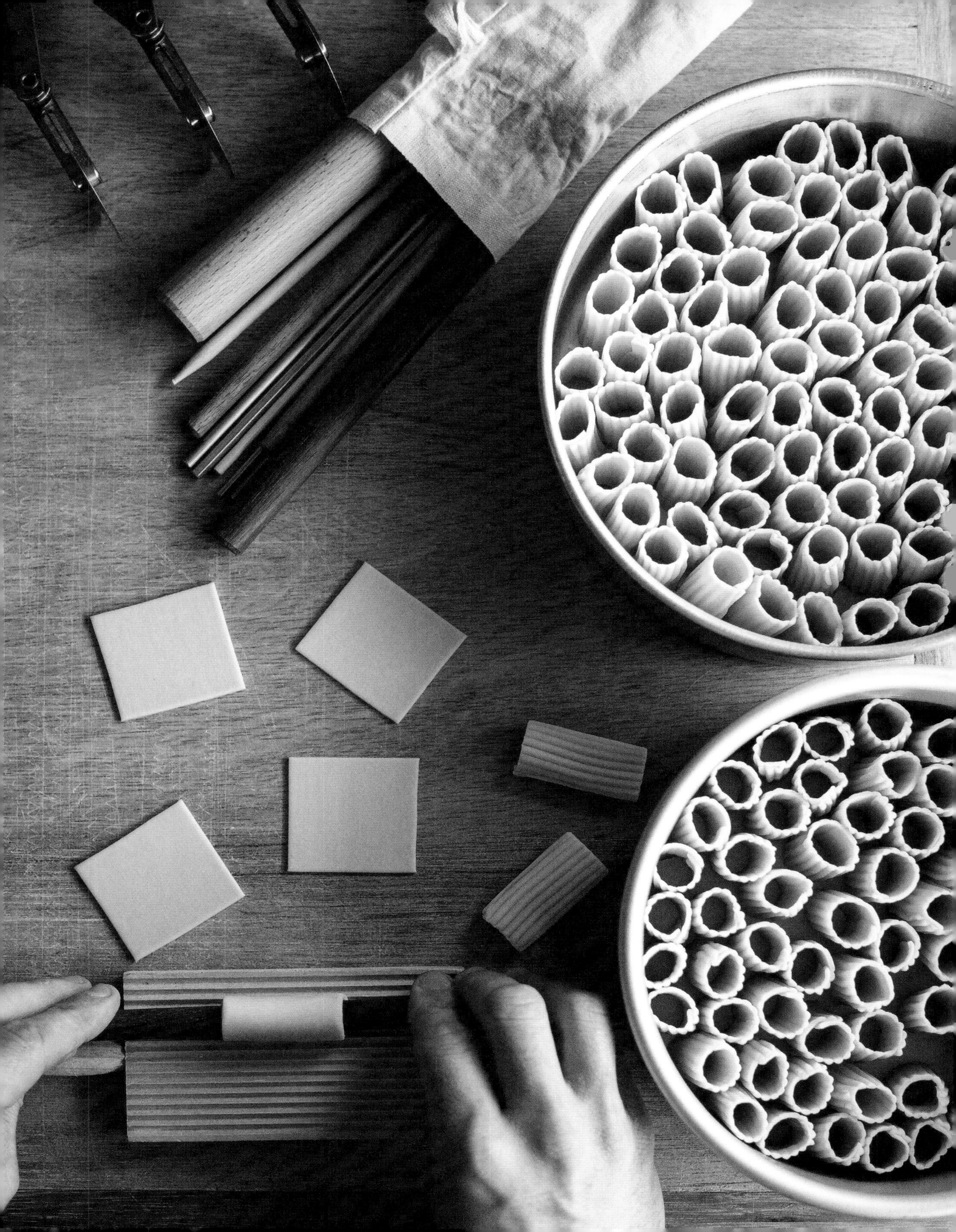

Rigatoni al forno

SERVES 6 | TOTAL TIME 2 HRS 30 MINS

There was often a uniquely delicious smell filling my great aunty's house when we'd drop by for a meal. I remember us cousins lolling about in the lounge room of her old heritage house before dinner, all seventies colours, velvet and a piano, breathing in the intoxicating smells of baked pasta. This is in contrast to my poor nonna, whose penchant for boiled broad beans left her house more often than not smelling like sweaty feet. Don't even get me started on the tripe.

It was many years before I learned that the characteristic ingredients of Zia's famous pasta bake (and to be fair, my nonna's equally famous polpettone) were in fact rather representative of southern Italian cooking in general: the humble hard-boiled egg and a chunk of salami. This is our ultimate pasta al forno, packed with tiny pork and veal meatballs, 'nduja, cacciatore Calabrese, hard-boiled eggs, provolone, pecorino Romano, chilli, tomatoes and a big old handful of spice. The flavours that defined my childhood and that tie us back to our family's dear Calabria.

1½ × quantities Whole egg dough (page 18)

MEATBALLS

250 g (9 oz) minced (ground) veal
250 g (9 oz) minced (ground) pork
35 g (1¼ oz) breadcrumbs
25 g (1 oz) Parmigiano Reggiano, grated
1 egg
½ teaspoon ground sage
½ teaspoon dried thyme
½ teaspoon dried rosemary
½ teaspoon hot paprika
½ teaspoon garlic powder
½ teaspoon onion powder
1 tablespoon extra-virgin olive oil

SAUCE

2 tablespoons extra-virgin olive oil
6–8 garlic cloves, roughly chopped
1 onion, diced
1 handful of basil leaves
1 small handful of sage leaves
2 teaspoons fennel seeds
700 ml (23½ fl oz) passata (puréed tomatoes)
1 teaspoon sugar
salt and freshly cracked black pepper, to taste
4 eggs
100 g (3½ oz) cacciatore Calabrese, sliced into half-discs
100 g (3½ oz) 'nduja
200 g (7 oz) provolone

Prepare 2 mm (⅛ in) thick sheets from the pasta dough, then cut and form into rigatoni (see Tube pasta: Tutorial, page 118).

Combine all the meatball ingredients, except the olive oil, in a bowl and use your hands to knead everything together like dough. Let it squeeze through your fingers. To save time, quickly divide the meatball mix into small grape-sized lumps before rolling them all into tiny meatballs between your palms. Heat the oil in a large heavy pot and fry the meatballs until a golden-brown crust begins to form. If you don't have a large pot, cook these in batches in a smaller one to avoid overcrowding. Remove the meatballs and set aside.

To make the sauce, drop the heat to low–medium and add 2 tablespoons of oil to the pot. Add the garlic and onion and cook, stirring, for 10 minutes, or until the onion has softened. Add the basil, sage and fennel seeds, and cook for a further 2–3 minutes, or until the basil has turned bright green and the herbs are aromatic. Pour in the passata, seasoning with the sugar, salt and pepper. Be sure to half-fill the empty passata bottle with water and swill around before pouring that into the pot. Reintroduce the meatballs, drop the heat to low and cook for 20 minutes, stirring occasionally.

Preheat the oven to 180°C (360°F). Add the eggs to a pot, cover with cold water and bring to the boil. Boil for 14 minutes, until hard, before removing and immersing in cold water. Remove the shells.

After 20 minutes, remove the sauce from the heat and stir through the cacciatore. Blanch the pasta in boiling water for 25–30 seconds, then drain before plunging into iced water. Break the 'nduja into small chunks and chop the provolone and hard-boiled eggs into cubes. Spoon a layer of sauce and pasta into a lasagne dish before sprinkling with 'nduja, provolone and egg. Repeat until all ingredients are used up, about 4–5 layers. Transfer the dish to the oven and cook for 30 minutes, or until the top layer of pasta begins to darken. Remove and allow to sit for a few minutes before serving.

ON PASTA

I reckon that if it's pasta, it can be al forno. That said, tube pasta like rigatoni, tortiglioni (see page 118), ziti or even penne are hard to beat baked. Conchiglie is another winner, otherwise you can push into stuffed territory with conchiglioni, paccheri or cannelloni (see page 118). If you want to go truly wild with something like a tortellini or orecchiette (see page 154) I'm not going to dampen your enthusiasm, just remember that you may need to adjust that initial blanch time before they hit the oven (particularly for something with a long cook time like orecchiette).

Note that you will struggle getting handmade tube pasta like this to hold its hollow shape. The drier the dough the better it'll hold as formed, but the harder it will be to roll without cracking. However, by stirring well before layering you will still get a delicious layer of sauce all caught up in it. If you're just about that gap, try out our extruded pasta recipe with a rigatoni cutter attached (see Extruded pasta: Tutorial, page 82).

ON INGREDIENTS

If you're not big on chilli, swap that 'nduja out for another cured meat. My family often used thinly sliced salami, which adds an extra bit of delicious crunch where it pokes out the top.

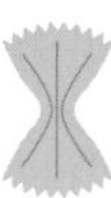

Tortiglioni with roasted zucchini and stracciatella

SERVES 4 | TOTAL TIME 35 MINS

One of my favourite flavour shortcuts is to roast a main ingredient in the oven before stirring it into a quick, or even uncooked sauce. Eggplant (aubergine), garlic, fennel and zucchini (courgette) are our top choices, giving the dish a little more depth than you'd achieve on the stovetop alone. This sauce pairs that roasted quality with the springy freshness of stracciatella for a creamy but pleasantly light sauce. As always, choose the freshest ingredients and let them do the work for you.

- 1 × quantity Whole egg and egg yolk dough (page 19)
- 4 zucchini (courgettes), chopped into rounds
- 80 ml (2½ fl oz/⅓ cup) extra-virgin olive oil
- 2 teaspoons garlic powder
- juice of ½ lemon
- 400 g (14 oz) stracciatella
- salt and freshly cracked black pepper, to taste

Roll the dough into 2 mm (⅛ in) thick sheets and form tortiglioni (see Tube pasta: Tutorial, page 118).

Heat the oven to 220°C (430°F). Toss the zucchini in the olive oil and garlic powder, and roast for 15 minutes until tender and beginning to brown. Transfer to a mixing bowl.

Boil the tortiglioni in a large pot of salted water for 4–5 minutes, testing for doneness. Scoop out, retaining a cup of pasta water, and drop directly into the mixing bowl with the zucchini. Stir well, adding the lemon juice and half of the stracciatella; pour a little of the pasta water in as necessary to assist emulsification. Season to taste.

Serve with the remaining stracciatella on top and a crack of black pepper.

ON PASTA

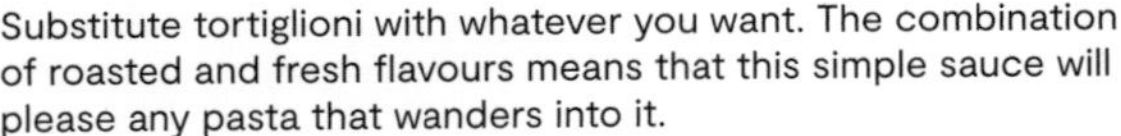

Substitute tortiglioni with whatever you want. The combination of roasted and fresh flavours means that this simple sauce will please any pasta that wanders into it.

ON INGREDIENTS

Every now and then I treat myself to a fresh burrata, and eat the outside with a few pieces of thinly sliced prosciutto while I stir the stracciatella filling into a fresh serve of pasta. Just saying.

BIG AND FLAT

Alongside hand-cut and filled varieties, sheet pasta like lasagne and rotolo feature regularly on our pasta rotation. There are simply few things as heart-warming as a tall slice of lasagne, or a rolled up and filled piece of pasta. We also have stuffed and baked fazzoletti, and hand-stamped corzetti. Though in no way exhaustive, this chapter offers a nice cross-section of the joys to be found amongst the most uncomplicated of pasta shapes: the big and the flat.

Green lasagne with bolognese

SERVES 8 | TOTAL TIME 6 HRS 50 MINS

One of the hardest, most gut-wrenching moments of my life coincided with one of the happiest. A few weeks after Elio was born, while I was still getting to know the cheery, relaxed little man, the boys almost lost their mum, and me my wife. There was a quiet in the house after the ambulance left that permanently cut a piece out of me.

Rach hung in there though. We eventually found a way to get Elio into the hospital to be with her, around pandemic visiting restrictions, and smuggled in under his pram we delivered her pasta. But in a way so perfectly typical of this incredible person, it was a green lasagne that Rachel herself had made and frozen for us weeks earlier, just in case.

This is not a traditional recipe, but it's one of Rachel's specialties and something that we've always cooked together: Rach on the sauce, Aldo and I making the pasta. All that I can say is savour the little moments like that, love each other, and always keep emergency pasta in the freezer.

1 × quantity Spinach dough (page 24)

200 g (7 oz) fresh mozzarella, thinly torn (substitute with shredded mozzarella)

BOLOGNESE

- 2 onions, diced
- 100 ml (3½ fl oz) extra-virgin olive oil
- 10 garlic cloves, minced
- 500 g (1 lb 2 oz) minced (ground) beef or veal
- 500 g (1 lb 2 oz) minced (ground) pork
- 2 carrots, finely grated
- 2 zucchini (courgettes), finely grated
- 200 ml (7 fl oz) wine, either red or white
- 140 g (5 oz) tomato paste (concentrated purée)
- 800 g (1 lb 12 oz) crushed tomatoes
- 800 g (1 lb 12 oz) tinned cherry tomatoes
- 1 teaspoon dried basil
- 1 teaspoon dried oregano
- 2 bay leaves
- pinch of nutmeg
- sugar, salt and freshly cracked black pepper, to taste

BÉCHAMEL

- 100 g (3½ oz) butter
- 80 g (2¾ oz) plain (all-purpose) flour
- 1 litre (34 fl oz/4 cups) full-cream (whole) milk
- 120 g (4½ oz) Parmigiano Reggiano, grated
- nutmeg, salt and freshly cracked black pepper, to taste

Begin the bolognese by gently sautéing the onion in the olive oil in a large, heavy-based pot over a low heat. Stir regularly until soft and golden, about 15–20 minutes.

Add the garlic, cook for 1–2 minutes, then stir in the meat, raising the heat to high. Cook until the meat has browned, 4–5 minutes.

Stir in the carrot and zucchini and cook for a further 10 minutes. Pour in the wine and let it cook off for a few minutes before adding in the tomato paste, crushed tomatoes and cherry tomatoes, along with the basil, oregano, bay leaves and nutmeg. Season to taste with sugar, salt and pepper, then bring to the boil before dropping the heat to low. Cook, partially covered, for 5–6 hours. Stir regularly, adding a little water if it becomes too thick and dry.

To prepare the béchamel, melt the butter in a saucepan over a medium–high heat until it begins to foam, then stir in the flour and cook for 2 minutes. Gradually pour in the milk, whisking vigorously, and cook for a further 5 minutes until thickened. Remove from the heat and stir in the Parmigiano Reggiano. Season to taste with freshly grated nutmeg, salt and pepper.

Preheat the oven to 180°C (360°F) and bring a large pot of salted water to the boil. Roll the pasta into sheets of 2 mm (⅛ in) thickness (see Handmade pasta: Tutorial, page 33), and cut to fit the length of your dish. Working in small batches, drop the pasta sheets into the boiling water for 30 seconds.

Spoon a thin covering of bolognese into the bottom of the lasagne dish, then lay the first pasta sheets, reaching to all edges. Note that you may need two side-by-side to cover the width of the dish. Add a layer of sauce, followed by béchamel and mozzarella. Repeat until you reach the top of the dish, finishing with mozzarella and a crack of black pepper.

Cover and bake for 45 minutes before uncovering and baking for a further 30 minutes. Allow to cool for 10–15 minutes before serving.

ON PASTA

There's no need to go green, and actually ours was often made with plain dough. You can also try thicker or thinner slices of dough, but remember to adjust your blanch time to suit. Aside from potentially ending up undercooked, thicker pasta that goes in too raw will draw more moisture out of the sauce, leaving it drier than you may have hoped (that said, you can always try compensating by using a wetter sauce).

ON INGREDIENTS

Due to the quantities that the bolognese ingredients are usually available in, this recipe will make up to one-fifth more sauce than you actually need. Either cut them down accordingly, or set a portion of bolognese aside for an easy dinner on another night.

Fazzoletti al forno

SERVES 4 | TOTAL TIME 1 HR 10 MINS

Fazzoletti, as the name suggests, are giant squares of pasta resembling handkerchiefs. The Abruzzesi have truly done the world a great service by deciding to stuff and bake them, and that's not something that I say lightly. My nonna, Calabrese, famously held a light-hearted but nonetheless persistent grudge against the Abruzzesi. No one really knows how it started, particularly given that plenty of family friends were in fact from Abruzzo, but my dad still chuckles to recount wedding speeches that all too often began with 'good evening ladies and gentlemen, friends and family, and Abruzzesi'.

This Abruzzese specialty, made with a mince and sausage ragù, thickened to a filling with the addition of egg, is sure to help you forgive (or at least temporarily forget) all but the most severe of regionally specific trespasses.

- 1 onion, diced
- 2 garlic cloves, finely chopped
- 2 tablespoons extra-virgin olive oil
- 400 g (14 oz) minced (ground) beef
- 200 g (7 oz) Italian sausage, squeezed out of the skins and crumbled
- 2 teaspoons dried red chilli flakes
- 1 teaspoon fennel seeds
- 100 ml (3½ fl oz) red wine
- 700 ml (23½ fl oz) passata (puréed tomatoes)
- salt and cracked black pepper, to taste
- 1 egg
- 100 g (3½ oz) pecorino Romano, grated, plus extra for topping the pasta
- 50 g (1¾ oz) fine breadcrumbs
- 1 × quantity Whole egg and egg yolk dough (page 19), made with half plain (all-purpose) flour and half wholemeal (whole-wheat) flour

Gently sauté the onion and garlic in the olive oil in a large frying pan over a low heat for 10–15 minutes until soft and fragrant. Stir regularly to prevent it from browning.

Raise the heat to medium–high and brown the mince and sausage for 3–4 minutes before adding the chilli and fennel seeds and stirring for a further minute. Deglaze with the wine and cook it off before pouring in the passata. Drop the heat to low–medium and season. Cook for 15–20 minutes, stirring occasionally.

Preheat the oven to 180°C (360°F) and bring a large pot of salted water to the boil. Transfer half of the meat sauce to a mixing bowl to cool. Add the egg, pecorino and breadcrumbs, and combine into a thick filling consistency. If too wet, add more breadcrumbs; too dry, add a little water.

Roll the pasta dough out into 2 mm (⅛ in) sheets (see Handmade Pasta: Tutorial, page 33), cutting it into squares. On a standard machine, these will be 15 cm (6 in) across. Blanch in the boiling water for 30 seconds; you may need to work in batches to avoid overcrowding.

Spread a large spoonful of filling across each square, then fold in half and half again, just like a handkerchief. Spoon half of the remaining sauce into the bottom of a small lasagne dish, lay the stuffed fazzoletti on top, then pour the remaining sauce over the top of them.

Add a little more pecorino on top, then bake for 15–20 minutes until the pasta begins to crisp. Serve with a little cracked black pepper.

ON PASTA

Sheet pasta is very well suited to having a higher ratio of wholemeal (whole-wheat) flour in it, if you're after that earthiness like us. By the same token, fazzoletti is a great opportunity to try out just about any dough you like, as it doesn't need shaping or even much slicing.

ON INGREDIENTS

Abruzzesi know lamb, so we sometimes do a delicious variation of this using minced (ground) lamb instead of beef and sausage. Toss in a few sprigs of rosemary, and maybe add some pancetta while the meat browns.

Spinach and ricotta rotolo with tomato and béchamel sauce

SERVES 4 | TOTAL TIME 1 HR 45 MINS

Unlike most of the family dishes in this book, I made this for the first time only a couple of years back after extensive correspondence with Ma, teasing the recipe out of her. She tells me that it's something she used to make for special occasions, before I was born. By which I take it nothing of particular note happened after that point.

There are a few different ways to make and serve rotolo, but ours is poached the traditional way, before being sliced and baked in a creamy tomato sauce. It is a bit fiddlier than our usual pasta, but well worth it.

1 × quantity Whole egg and egg yolk dough (page 19)

PASTA FILLING

- 500 g (1 lb 2 oz/10 cups) fresh spinach, washed
- 1 onion, chopped
- 1 tablespoon extra-virgin olive oil
- 6 large slices prosciutto, finely chopped
- 300 g (10½ oz) fresh ricotta
- 100 g (3½ oz) pecorino Romano, grated
- 1 egg yolk
- ¼ teaspoon ground nutmeg
- salt and freshly cracked black pepper, to taste

SUGO

- 2 tablespoons extra-virgin olive oil
- 1 onion, finely diced
- 1 small handful of basil leaves
- 700 ml (23½ fl oz) passata (puréed tomatoes)
- ½ teaspoon sugar
- salt, to taste

BÉCHAMEL

- 25 g (1 oz) butter
- 20 g (¾ oz) plain (all-purpose) flour
- 250 ml (8½ fl oz/1 cup) full-cream (whole) milk
- 30 g (1 oz) Parmigiano Reggiano, grated

To make the filling, wilt the spinach for 3–4 minutes in a frying pan over a medium heat with only the water left from washing it; remove and finely chop.

Sauté the onion in the oil over a medium heat until pale, around 8 minutes, then add the prosciutto and cook over a high heat for a further 3 minutes. Transfer to a mixing bowl to cool before stirring in the spinach, ricotta, pecorino, egg yolk and nutmeg, then season.

To poach the rotolo, bring a large stockpot of lightly salted water (two-thirds full) to the boil and preheat the oven to 200°C (390°F). Cut the dough in half and roll it out into long sheets about 15 cm (6 in) wide and 1.5 mm (1⁄16 in) thick (see Handmade pasta: Tutorial, page 33).

Spread the filling evenly over the pasta sheets, then roll up by the short edges. Wrap each roll tightly in a tea towel (dish towel) or a piece of muslin (cheesecloth), tying with kitchen twine, and then poach for 20 minutes in the salted water. Remove and allow to cool before unwrapping.

For the sugo, add the oil and onion to a cold frying pan set over a low–medium heat. Stir regularly, until the onion begins to sweat and turn translucent, approximately 10 minutes.

Bruise the basil lightly and add to the pan. Cook for a further minute before adding the passata, sugar and a pinch of salt. Simmer gently for 15 minutes, until thickened, then remove from the heat.

To make the béchamel, melt the butter in a saucepan over a medium–high heat until it begins to foam, then stir in the flour and cook for 2 minutes. Gradually pour in the milk, whisking vigorously, and cook for a further 5 minutes until thickened. Remove from the heat and stir in the Parmigiano Reggiano. Season to taste, then stir into the sugo.

Chop the cooled rotolo into slices of approximately 2 cm (¾ in) thickness. Spoon a layer of sauce into the bottom of a baking dish, then stand the rotolo slices up on an angle, dolloping the remaining sauce in between and on top. Bake for 20–25 minutes until the sauce begins to crack and the pasta edges start to brown.

ON PASTA

If you're just not in the mood for all of that rolling and poaching, use the same filling inside cannelloni (see page 118). You can make them quite easily by blanching large rectangular sheets of fresh pasta before laying the filling across them and rolling them up.

ON INGREDIENTS

When tying it all up, we use a similar technique to what you would with a roast. Twist the tea towel (dish towel) closed on either side of the rotolo and then tie one end firmly closed with the twine. Form a loop around your fingers (with a little twist to keep it closed) and thread it on over the top of the sealed end. Don't tighten excessively. Continue to add loops in this manner, always working from the knotted end, until the whole rotolo is wrapped. Tie it off and you're good to go.

Corzetti

Corzetti are a simple pasta made elegant through the use of beautiful and varied hand-carved stamps. If you don't have a corzetti stamp, you can approximate this pasta with a cookie cutter and cookie stamp.

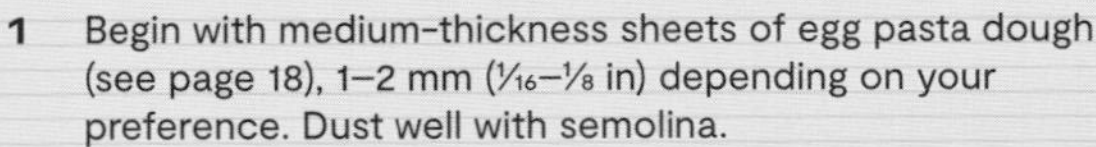

1 Begin with medium-thickness sheets of egg pasta dough (see page 18), 1–2 mm (1/16–1/8 in) depending on your preference. Dust well with semolina.

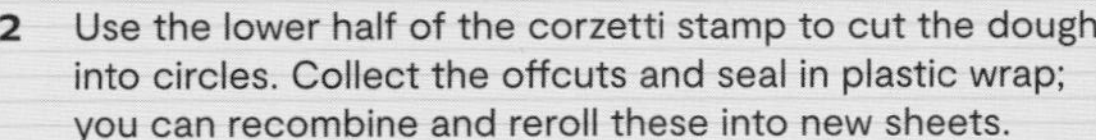

2 Use the lower half of the corzetti stamp to cut the dough into circles. Collect the offcuts and seal in plastic wrap; you can recombine and reroll these into new sheets.

3 Place a circle of dough between the two inner moulds of the corzetti stamp and press down to imprint both sides.

4 Remove, and lay flat to dry.

Blue corzetti with mint and mountain pepper

SERVES 4 | TOTAL TIME 35 MINS

Corzetti, a Ligurian specialty, are exactly what they look like: stamped pasta. During the Renaissance, families began printing their coats of arms onto their pasta, a sentiment that I can get behind, and an industry was born for these beautiful hand-carved tools and the ornate carbs that they produce.

Steeped as they are in tradition and history, we had to do something playful; so we've made our corzetti blue and purple. Butterfly pea flower releases a deep blue colour when steeped, which becomes a brilliant magenta with the addition of citric acid, and then a soft purple when mixed into an egg dough like this.

- 1 × quantity Whole egg dough (page 18), made with 20 g (¾ oz) butterfly pea flower; half of that made with ½ teaspoon citric acid (see page 21)
- 100 g (3½ oz) butter
- 2 native mint sprigs
- ½ tablespoon mountain pepper berries, lightly crushed
- sea salt flakes, to serve

Roll the dough into sheets of 1–2 mm (1⁄16–⅛ in) thickness (see Handmade pasta: Tutorial, page 33). Form into corzetti (see Corzetti: Tutorial, page 134).

Melt the butter in a saucepan over a medium–high heat for 3–5 minutes, stirring constantly. You'll see it bubble and foam as the butter begins to brown.

As the butter gets hotter and the foam starts to dissipate, add the native mint and mountain pepper, and continue to stir for another 1–2 minutes.

Once the foam has disappeared, the rate of browning will increase rapidly. Keep a close eye on it, tasting as the colour deepens, until it reaches your desired flavour.

Boil the pasta in a large pot of salted water for 3–4 minutes until done. Scoop out and toss gently in the pan with the brown butter before serving with a sprinkling of salt flakes.

ON PASTA

Regular, uncoloured dough works too and, in fact, a rich egg yolk dough goes brilliantly with a butter sauce like this.

ON INGREDIENTS

I personally love the deep, regal colours that you get by mixing butterfly pea flower into an egg yolk dough, and I enjoy this richer dough for corzetti. That said, the yellow yolks will make it all a bit green. For punchier colours, try butterfly pea flower in an eggless dough. Also note that you can change the pasta's colour by adding acidity to your pasta water instead of the dough; it just requires more of it given the quantity of water, and is a bit harder to measure for.

To serve, we've opted for a couple of native Aussie flavours. If you can get them, they're definitely worth trying. I'm particularly obsessed with mountain pepper berries, but keep in mind that (as with many native ingredients) a little goes a long way.

SMALL
AND
SQUISHY

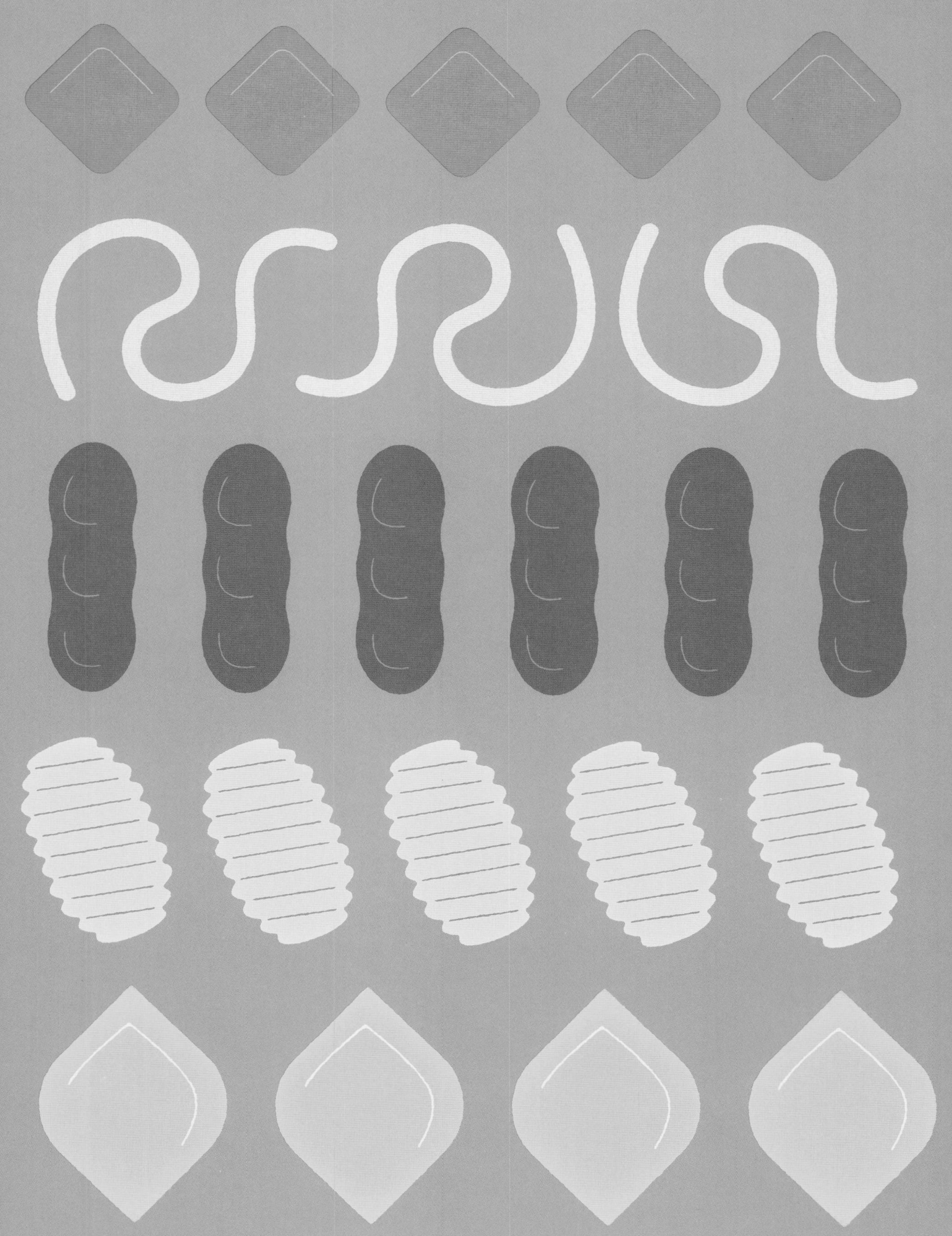

A significant consideration in deciding the structure of this book was the opportunity to pen a chapter entitled 'Small and squishy'. This section contains some of the easiest and also most satisfying of pasta shapes: a selection of our favourite eggless pasta, and a couple of sneaky gnocchi recipes. More specifically, malloreddus, capunti, casarecce, orecchiette, foglie d'ulivo, gnocchi ripieni and gnudi.

These are forgiving shapes, perfect for learning through trial and error, and for embracing a certain rustic inconsistency in the final product. They're also some of the first pasta shapes that Aldo and Elio learned, which seems appropriate given that both went through a 'gnocco' stage at a few weeks of age where, wrapped up tightly in muslins, they were largely indistinguishable from potato dumplings.

Put on some classic and clichéd Italian music, find yourself a comfy bit of benchtop (or an al fresco table for that true nonna experience), and embrace the simpler pleasures of the pasta world.

TUTORIAL

Malloreddus, capunti

These are two fantastically simple, rustic pasta shapes, made in a similar manner to each other.

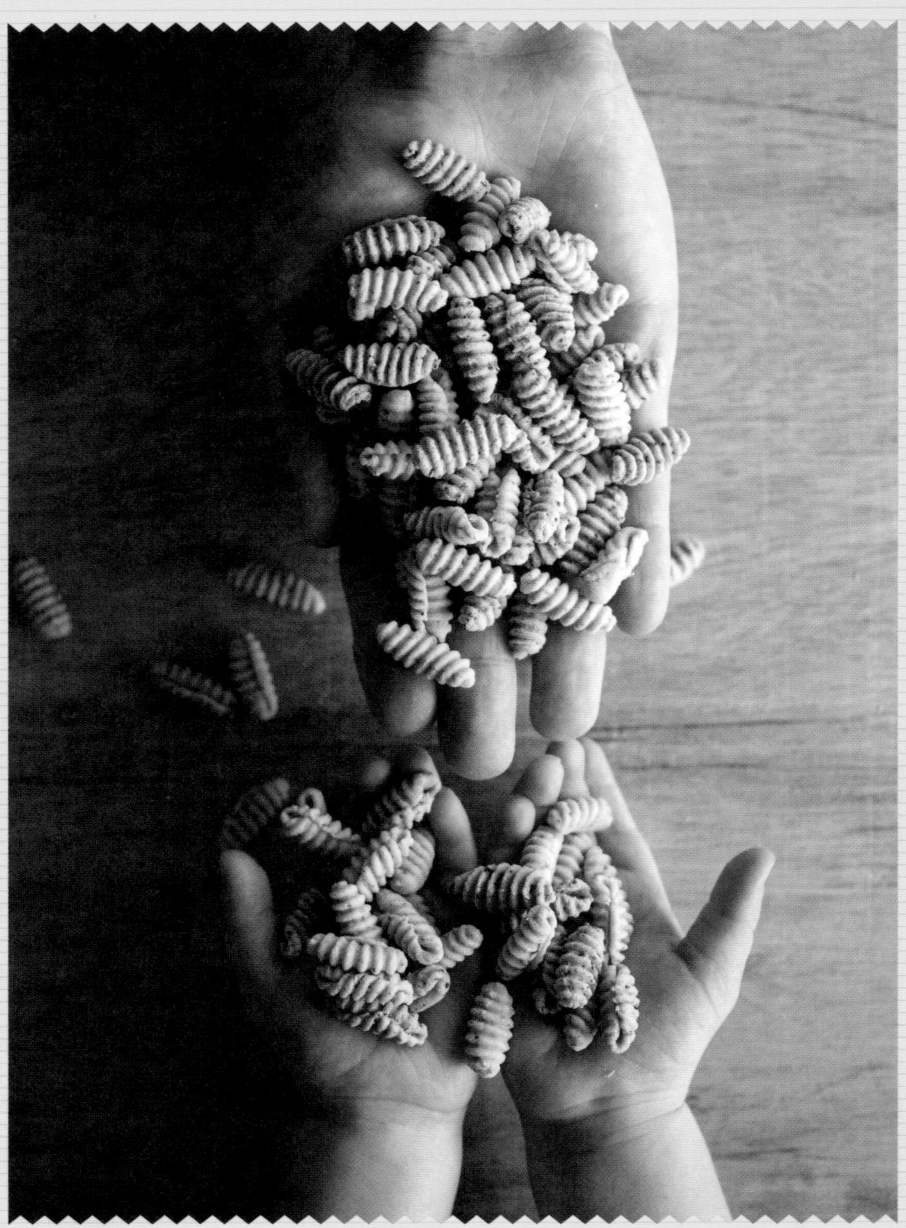

1 For malloreddus, roll an eggless pasta dough (see page 22) out into long, thin ropes, around 1 cm (½ in) in diameter. Cover any dough that you're not immediately working on to prevent it drying out.

2 Chop the ropes into small 1–1.5 cm (½ in) sized pieces.

3 Use a cavarola or gnocchi board, the back of a flat grater, or the underside of a fork to shape into malloreddus. To do so, roll each piece away from yourself, providing just enough downward pressure to imprint the dough as it folds over itself. A bench scraper will provide a crisper shape, but thumbs and fingers always worked for the nonne.

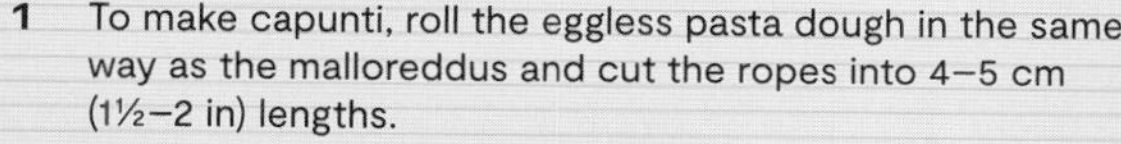

1 To make capunti, roll the eggless pasta dough in the same way as the malloreddus and cut the ropes into 4–5 cm (1½–2 in) lengths.

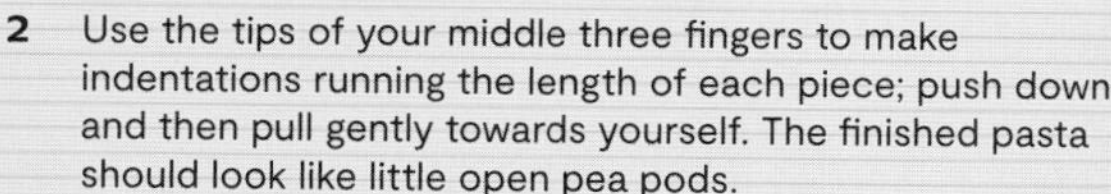

2 Use the tips of your middle three fingers to make indentations running the length of each piece; push down and then pull gently towards yourself. The finished pasta should look like little open pea pods.

Wattleseed and peppermint gum malloreddus with sea celery and macadamia pesto

SERVES 4 | TOTAL TIME 45 MINS

The Italian-Australian experience, and all that it brings with it, is actually the only 'Italian' that I've ever known. My brother and I grew up with an Italian mum (first-generation Australian) and an English-Australian dad, spending most of our early years in the care of a thoroughly Calabrian nonna who arrived in that rich fifties boom. To this day, the only Italian that sounds right to me is her comfortable, lazy southern drawl, and the only Italian-English accent that makes sense comes from that same familiar dialect. Likewise, the food, customs and characters that I grew up knowing first as just family, and then later as 'Italian', are actually part of this unique transplanted blend of cultures. And I know that we're not alone.

With this pasta, we wanted to create a dish that really allowed Italian to meet Australian. In particular, some of those true native flavours that are so well known to this country's First Peoples, yet rarely make it into home recipes. I think that many of us Aussies feel an affinity with the natural world around us; with the shapes of its leaves, the ochre of its earth, the air, the animals. But its original Owners hold a relationship with this land that spans tens of thousands of years, from long before outsiders declared it 'terra nullius' and disingenuously invited my ancestors in two centuries later. I want our boys to grow up developing their own love and appreciation for what we have today, but also with a clear understanding of what brought us here. And of course, in part, we pass on ideas and history through food. So, we made this little dish.

To the Ngunnawal and Whadjuk Peoples, we acknowledge you as the Traditional Custodians of the magnificent and unceded land on which we tell this tale through food. Our deepest respects to your Elders past and present.

- ½ × quantity Semolina dough, (page 22), made with 2 teaspoons ground wattleseed (see page 23)
- ½ × quantity Semolina dough, (page 22), made with 1 teaspoon ground peppermint gum (see page 23)
- 120 g (4½ oz/¾ cup) roasted macadamia nuts
- 80 g (2¾ oz) basil
- 80 ml (2½ fl oz/⅓ cup) extra-virgin olive oil
- 60 g (2 oz) pecorino Romano, grated
- 2 large garlic cloves, peeled
- 6 large sea celery sprigs
- 4 large seablite sprigs (if seasonally unavailable, thinner-leafed varieties of saltbush are a great substitution)
- 8–10 native mint leaves (plus another 12–16 fried leaves for plating)
- 2 mountain pepper leaves
- 6–8 mountain pepper berries, cracked, for plating

Roll the doughs into ropes of about 1 cm (½ in) in diameter, chop into 1 cm (½ in) long pieces and form into malloreddus (see Malloreddus, capunti: Tutorial, page 142).

To make the pesto, add all the remaining ingredients to a mortar and pestle and pound until mostly smooth with some chunks, or to your desired consistency. For a greener colour, finely chop the leafy ingredients beforehand.

Drop the malloreddus into boiling water and cook for 4–5 minutes, or until al dente. Note that the larger you make your pasta, the longer they will take to cook (up to 20 minutes for grape-sized balls). You'll know they're ready if still firm but showing no white dough when cut into. Drain, retaining a little of the pasta water, and toss into the pesto. If needed, add some pasta water to aid emulsification. Serve with cracked mountain pepper berries.

ON PASTA

These are such excellent, bitey little things, but can be easily substituted with anything you'd normally find tossed in pesto. Foglie d'ulivo (see page 154) or fazzoletti (tossed unfolded through the pesto) would be amongst my first choices.

ON INGREDIENTS

If you have access to native Australian ingredients, but not these exact ones, have a little play around and see what you can do. Milder plants like warrigal greens, saltbush, or even pigface can stand in for seablite, but you will lose a distinctive hit of flavour by swapping out the sea celery. If none of this is available to you, build a more classic pesto for now and add edible Aussie natives to your 'must-try' list.

Red wine capunti with sausage and broccoli rabe

SERVES 4 | TOTAL TIME 1 HR 5 MINS

You'd think that an Italian family would be big wine drinkers, but ours was an Aussie if-not-born-of-the-bush-then-drink-like-it kind of bunch: the cheapest, roughest cans of locally produced beer, occasionally swirled into a good old shandy. If there was wine around it would be an equally rough marsala to cook with, or the occasional bottle of someone's suspiciously unlabelled home-made endeavour. The great uncles did make grappa, of course, the sweet smell of stills installed in spare bathrooms wafting over the Perth hills every Sunday morning, but when we sat down to a meal it was all beer. Wine was yet another thing that I didn't associate with 'Italian' until I was much older.

I've made up for it since then, straight-up mixing wine into my pasta dough. In order to really capture the flavour and colour, boil it right down to around one-quarter of its original volume before swapping it into the wet ingredients. The eggless dough has a softness that goes perfectly with the wine's flavour. Served here simply with sausage, broccoli rabe and cheese.

- 1 × quantity eggless Red wine dough (page 23)
- 4–6 garlic cloves, finely chopped
- 1 onion, diced
- 60 ml (2 fl oz/¼ cup) extra-virgin olive oil
- 400 g (14 oz) Italian sausage
- 400 g (14 oz) broccoli rabe, blanched and finely chopped
- 40 g (1½ oz) pecorino Romano, grated, to serve
- freshly cracked black pepper, to serve

Roll the dough out into long ropes of approximately 1 cm (½ in) in diameter. Chop into 4–5 cm (1½–2 in) lengths and form into capunti (see Malloreddus, capunti: Tutorial, page 142).

Sauté the garlic and onion in the olive oil in a large frying pan over a low–medium heat for 10 minutes, or until soft and fragrant.

Increase the heat to medium–high. Squeeze the sausages out of their casings and crumble into the pan. Cook, stirring, for 10–15 minutes until they begin to turn brown and crispy. Stir in the chopped broccoli rabe and cook for a further 5–6 minutes until soft.

Boil the capunti in salted water for 4–5 minutes, check for doneness, and then scoop directly into the frying pan with the sauce, retaining a cup of pasta water. Stir well, adding enough pasta water to help the sauce and pasta combine.

Serve with grated pecorino and cracked black pepper.

ON PASTA

Swap out these capunti for any eggless pasta. Orecchiette (see page 154) is a great choice.

ON INGREDIENTS

For something that grows on railway tracks, it can be surprisingly hard to find broccoli rabe. You can sometimes buy it frozen, but otherwise any leafy green will work in its place.

TUTORIAL

Casarecce

This simple pasta is a quick and delightful shape, smooth and firm, with a grooved surface perfect for collecting all of your saucy goodness.

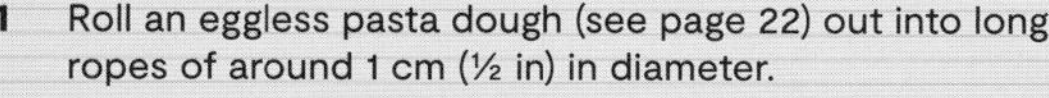

1 Roll an eggless pasta dough (see page 22) out into long ropes of around 1 cm (½ in) in diameter.

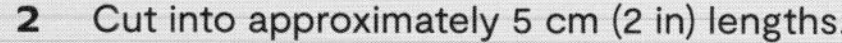

2 Cut into approximately 5 cm (2 in) lengths.

3 Align a ferretto, narrow dowel, or knitting needle horizontally along each piece of pasta, slightly off-centre and roll gently towards one edge. Apply gentle downward pressure as you go, so that the dough rolls slightly up and around the dowel.

4 Allow it to flip, and then lay a second dowel over the turned-over dough. Roll both together, shaping the dough into an s-shape around them. Slide free.

NOTE For a simpler method, producing a c-shape, press a dowel once into the centre of each length.

Casarecce with tequila prawns and chorizo

SERVES 4 | TOTAL TIME 1 HR 50 MINS

Casarecce is a straightforward favourite, and a great pasta to get little hands involved with. Eggless dough in general is quite forgiving, and can be recombined, reshaped and rehydrated if necessary. This makes shapes like malloreddus (see page 142), pici (see page 66), fileja (see page 76) and capunti (see page 142) excellent choices for a bit of guided participation with very small children. For those wanting a little more challenge though, casarecce adds just the right amount of extra skill. It's a simple tool and technique to introduce and little Al was cranking these out by 18 months, albeit his own rustic versions. Being a second child, encouraged by his older brother's deliberately casual competence, Elio had a crack at 5 months. I recommend that in this circumstance you keep one ferretto for the pasta and one for chewing, and prepare yourself for an uneven distribution of labour.

Of course, for adults, an easy eggless pasta is a little simple therapy, akin to taking thirty minutes for some colouring-in, or luxuriating in a soft and pernicious smile over your cappuccino as someone else's child melts down across the café from you. This recipe is a non-traditional pasta sauce but a nonetheless timeless combination of flavours: good old prawn (shrimp) and chorizo.

- 1 × quantity 00 and semolina dough (page 22)
- 400 g (14 oz) school prawns (shrimp), shelled and deveined
- 60 ml (2 fl oz/¼ cup) tequila
- 2 garlic cloves, minced
- 2 tablespoons lime juice
- 1 teaspoon finely chopped coriander (cilantro), plus extra to serve
- 1 large red chilli, finely chopped
- 2 tablespoons extra-virgin olive oil
- 200 g (7 oz) chorizo, finely diced
- 200 g (7 oz) vine-ripened tomatoes, roughly chopped
- freshly cracked black pepper and sea salt flakes, to serve

Hand-roll the dough into ropes of about 1 cm (½ in) in diameter; cut to lengths of 5 cm (2 in) and form into casarecce (see Casarecce: Tutorial, page 148).

Marinate the prawns with the tequila, garlic, lime juice, coriander and red chilli for 1 hour, refrigerated.

Drain the prawns, retaining the marinade, and fry in 1 tablespoon olive oil over a medium–high heat for 5–7 minutes. Once they've coloured the whole way through and begun to brown, remove from the heat.

Into the same pan, add the remaining olive oil and fry the chorizo until crispy, 4–5 minutes. Deglaze with a little of the retained prawn marinade, then add the tomatoes. Cook for a further 10 minutes, stirring.

Boil the casarecce in a large pot of salted water for 4–5 minutes. Check for doneness then drain, retaining a cup of pasta water.

Combine the sauce, prawns and pasta in the frying pan, using a little pasta water to aid emulsification. Serve with a little more finely chopped coriander, a crack of black pepper and salt flakes.

ON PASTA

As with most eggless pasta, any other eggless pasta will usually work in its place. This also works well with long pasta, like spaghetti alla chitarra (see page 34).

ON INGREDIENTS

Substitute the prawns (shrimp) for any other fresh, white seafood. You can even make the casarecce longer or shorter depending on how chunky your substitution is.

Wholemeal casarecce with vodka tomato sauce

SERVES 4 | TOTAL TIME 55 MINS

At what point does a non-traditional dish become a classic? Pasta et Al is hardly one to actually care – as long as you enjoy it, cook it – but I think that Italian-American inventions like the old vodka tomato sauce have been around and loved for long enough to warrant a mention here as a classic. There's a smooth, glossy something to this dish that really hits the spot in a unique way. To those in uproar over cooking pasta with cream, firstly: get over it; secondly, we may actually have a sneaky preference for mascarpone anyway. Do whatever makes you happy.

As with many of these simpler sauces, we enjoy a heartier, earthier pasta dough, so we've gone for wholemeal (whole-wheat). Formed with the double-fold, these tasty little casarecce slurp in all that velvety goodness.

- 1 × quantity 00 and semolina dough (page 22), made with wholemeal (whole-wheat) flour in place of semolina
- 3 garlic cloves, minced
- 1 onion, finely diced
- 2 tablespoons extra-virgin olive oil
- 1 handful of fresh basil leaves
- 200 ml (7 fl oz) passata (puréed tomatoes)
- sugar, salt and freshly cracked black pepper, to taste
- 80 ml (2½ fl oz/⅓ cup) vodka
- 100 ml (3½ fl oz) thickened (whipping) cream or mascarpone
- grated hard cheese, to serve

Roll the dough into long ropes of 1 cm (½ in) in diameter and then cut into 5 cm (2 in) lengths; form casarecce (see Casarecce: Tutorial, page 148).

Gently sauté the garlic and onion in the olive oil in a large frying pan over a medium heat for 4–5 minutes until fragrant but not browning. Crush the basil leaves in your hands, then add to the frying pan for another 30–45 seconds until a vibrant green.

Stir in the passata, seasoning with a pinch of sugar and salt as required, and cook for 10–15 minutes until thick and halved in volume.

Pour the vodka into the tomato sauce and allow it to cook for 2–3 minutes until mostly evaporated.

Boil the casarecce in a large pot of salted water for 4–5 minutes until done. Drain and retain a cup of pasta water.

In a mixing bowl, gradually stir around half a cup of pasta water into the cream. This will help it come up to temperature without splitting. Pour this into the frying pan and stir to combine.

Add the casarecce to the sauce, using a little pasta water as required to bring it together.

Serve with grated cheese and cracked pepper.

ON PASTA

This is a sauce that pairs really well with both short and long pasta. Give it a try with bucatini (see page 82) or spaghetti (see page 34).

ON INGREDIENTS

It seems that I like casarecce with a bit of booze in the sauce, but you can leave out the alcohol for a simple tomato and cream sauce.

Orecchiette, foglie d'ulivo

Both of these shapes are made with eggless doughs, the semolina flour providing a wonderful texture.

1 For orecchiette, begin with long ropes of dough (see page 22), about 1 cm (½ in) in diameter; chop them into 1 cm (½ in) lengths.

2 Using a butter knife (not too sharp), lay it at 45 degrees to the top edge of each piece and then drag it towards you. Apply enough downward pressure to curl the dough up and over the knife. If required, use your thumb to completely turn the resulting pasta inside-out, with the rough textured side sticking out.

1 Foglie d'ulivo is much the same, but with longer pieces of dough and traditionally green in colour. Begin with pasta ropes of no more than 1 cm (½ in) in diameter; chop them into lengths of about 4 cm (1½ in).

2 Roll each piece between your hands to taper the ends.

3 Lay each piece vertically on your pasta board. Drag a blunt knife down the length of pasta, towards yourself, holding on to one end as you go. Apply more pressure in the centre to stretch it into a leaf shape.

NOTE Personally, I find it easier to lay the tapered dough at 45 degrees, then drag the knife parallel to its edge, away from myself. One of the joys in shaping pasta is discovering your own little preferences and techniques, so just see what works for you.

Orecchiette with broccoli and potato

SERVES 4 | TOTAL TIME 55 MINS

Broccoli and potato is a reminder for me of how powerful smells can be in holding and evoking memories. It's one of those beloved smells of my childhood, like the cool, swirling mix of fragrances that I remember hitting my face as I swatted my way through the plastic curtains of the wholefoods shop. Or the hallowed combination of tomatoes, salami and diesel from Nonna's garage.

It references a time not only in my life, but in the lives of the old Italians around me. You'd go to the shops, and still see old men sprawled around tables in the food court, sipping espressos in a garishly contrasting throwback to their Italian coffee shops. Then you'd go back to Nonna's and some variation of beans, broccoli or potato would be simmering on the stove. They're the kinds of flavours that we always love, cooked until soft, but then served with firm pasta. A lesson in not overcomplicating things.

- 1 × quantity Semolina dough (page 22)
- 400 g (14 oz) potato, cubed
- 600 g (1 lb 5 oz) broccoli, chopped into small pieces
- 3 tablespoons extra-virgin olive oil
- 1 teaspoon dried red chilli flakes
- 100 g (3½ oz) Parmigiano Reggiano, grated, plus extra to serve
- zest of 1 lemon, plus lemon juice to serve
- salt and freshly cracked black pepper, to taste

Roll the dough out into long ropes, then cut into pieces around 1 × 1 cm (½ × ½ in). Form into orecchiette (see Orecchiette, foglie d'ulivo: Tutorial, page 154).

Place the potato in a large pot and cover with cold water. Bring to the boil over a medium heat and cook until tender, around 15 minutes. Drain.

Boil the broccoli in a large pot of salted water for 2–3 minutes. Drain well and then fry with 2 tablespoons of the olive oil and the chilli in a large pan over a high heat for 3–4 minutes, or until the broccoli begins to brown. Blitz in a food processor with the remaining olive oil, cheese and lemon zest. Season to taste.

Cook the orecchiette in a large pot of salted water for 8–10 minutes. Note that it may take longer if you have made them thicker; always check that there's no raw white dough visible when you bite or cut into one. Drain, retaining a cup of pasta water.

Stir together the hot pasta, broccoli pesto and potato in a large mixing bowl. Use a little of the retained pasta water to bring it together if too dry.

Serve with freshly grated cheese and black pepper, and a little squeeze of lemon juice to taste.

ON PASTA

Pici (see page 66) and spaghetti (see page 34) are solid substitutes, as are most eggless pasta shapes.

ON INGREDIENTS

Boiling and then frying the broccoli, and even blending it, is a personal preference. For a simpler and lazier method, just boil the broccoli until soft and then stir it directly into the pasta with the remaining ingredients.

Foglie d'ulivo with pesto genovese

SERVES 4 | TOTAL TIME 35 MINS

We used to have a lone olive tree growing amongst the thick, otherwise native, bushland of our backyard. It was somewhat symbolic of the old Italian uncles who had recast themselves as Aussie men of the bush, orchardists, stubbornly pursuing their dreams of living and working off the land. Most striking surrounded by the earthy colours and wild geometry of hakeas and eucalypts were the olive's pale, subtly curled leaves.

This gorgeous pasta, inspired by those leaves, is a specialty of Puglia. Shaped much like stretched orecchiette (see page 154), here they are served with a simple, traditionally paired pesto.

- 1 × quantity Semolina dough (page 22)
- 60 g (2 oz/2 cups) basil leaves, finely chopped
- 100 ml (3½ fl oz) extra-virgin olive oil
- 60 g (2 oz) pecorino Romano, grated
- 40 g (1½ oz/¼ cup) pine nuts
- 2 small garlic cloves, minced
- salt and freshly cracked black pepper, to taste

Form the dough into long ropes around 1 cm (½ in) thick, then cut into 4 cm (1½ in) lengths. Shape into foglie d'ulivo (see Orecchiette, foglie d'ulivo: Tutorial, page 154).

Combine all the remaining ingredients in a mortar and pestle, grinding to a paste. Coarseness is really personal preference. Alternatively, blitz carefully in a food processor, ensuring that it doesn't become too runny.

Boil the pasta in a large pot of salted water for 8–10 minutes, or until no longer raw but still firm. Transfer to a mixing bowl, retaining one cup of pasta water.

Stir the pesto into the hot pasta using a little pasta water to thin out the sauce and properly coat the pasta.

Serve with a little cracked black pepper.

ON PASTA

Yes, ours are a heavier duty leaf than you'd find hanging on your typical olive tree, but each to their own. Use smaller pieces of dough for a more traditional, refined shape, and substitute with orecchiette (see page 154) or fazzoletti (tossed unfolded through the pesto).

ON INGREDIENTS

This is our basic pesto recipe. Get creative and experiment with a variety of nuts and greens until you find your own pesto groove.

On loss

Part of our story, and the stories that attach themselves to all food traditions, is loss. Even without knowing the history, as you carry on a tradition that's been passed on for hundreds of years, you can feel the people and places lost alongside it.

I wouldn't be the only grandchild to remember a nonna clad exclusively in black. We'd joke about it, and I think the cousins shared genuine shock when she one day emerged in colour, but she was living out loss, the act itself a carry-over from a homeland and community lost long before. My nonno passed away when I was very young, and this is what she was mourning. I knew her only in black for most of my early life. Though it seemed a little ridiculous at the time, looking back there's something beautiful about honouring a person you love by changing a little part of yourself. Her black clothing was a lived remembrance, and the stories that it sustained helped me feel like I grew up knowing him.

As we stood side by side making pasta, Nonna would also talk about him. He was strong, loved poetry, valued education. But he was also a joker: he would laugh often, sing nonsense verses and encourage mischief. Many years after his stroke, we found a 50-cent coin in a pair of my overalls that he'd given me to go and scratch his brother-in-law's car (I was less than 8 months old at the time). The cousins even remember Nonna at some point breaking from her stern and sombre character over her wobbly laminated pasta table to demonstrate how he would, in his baker years, roll his dough into huge absurd phalluses.

My nonna has always been different things to different people. By many accounts she was not always particularly happy and often quite harsh, but to the grandkids who spent so many of our early years with her, she was one of the very first lenses through which we saw the world (and she'd softened for our generation). The stories that she told, the pasta that we made, tied us to something far bigger than ourselves.

Me and Nonno

Nonna meeting Aldo

Me with Nonna, Ma, and Bisnonna

'Bittersweet though it is, Nonna is now and forever a part of that story that we tell when we make pasta.'

In the time that I've been away from Perth, dementia has largely taken Nonna. When I visit her now, there's sometimes a glimmer of recognition, a smile or a tear, but I'll never be able to truly tell her who I've become. Or that I have two sons now who make the same pasta with me that we made together decades earlier. Or that I've written a book about it. I can keep making pasta though, and with it I honour her and Nonno – everyone who came before them. Sometimes we even break out the knotted handkerchief hats that I remember her donning for a big day of cooking. Bittersweet though it is, Nonna is now and forever a part of that story that we tell when we make pasta.

More than seventy years have passed since that wave of migrants began to arrive, building their rich and beautiful pockets of Italy within Australia. And so now we are seeing the last of a generation disappear. With them we lose not only the last migrant nonni, the last living links to that part of our past, but also the unique blended culture that grew with them abroad. Languages and dialects alive here but disappearing back in Italy, sensibilities that we good-heartedly mocked and then fiercely loved just in time to lose, and whole communities who arrived with that bold Italian-Australian dream and saw it through.

Me and Nonna

We have our monuments, but sometimes they feel a little too still to celebrate life. And we have our history books, but they largely rest on shelves. Food is really how we remember – something that we actively create and revisit every single day. You don't need to make pasta, just sit down with whoever you have for a meal; remember those who aren't there, and love those who are.

Gnocchi, gnudi

Gnocchi, the honorary pasta. Though it's truly a potato dumpling, the close association and often interchangeability with pasta earns it a fleeting but heartfelt place in our book.

Our included recipe is for stuffed gnocchi, but it uses the exact same dough that we make our regular gnocchi from (see page 25).

GNOCCHI

1 Roast the potatoes for 40 minutes at 200°C (390°F). Note that here we're using a blue-purple variety. Once cool enough to handle but still warm, peel off the skins and pass the flesh through a potato ricer. Spread out to allow any excess moisture to evaporate.

2 Next, fold the cheese, flour, egg, and salt and pepper into the potato. Knead for 1–2 minutes before wrapping in plastic wrap and refrigerating for 30 minutes.

3 To shape, roll the dough into a long sausage of 1–2 cm (½–¾ in) in diameter; chop into pieces of the same length.

4 You can either leave them as is, poke a hollow in each with your thumb, or use a finger to drag them along the length of a gnocchi board. Apply gentle downward pressure as you go, allowing the gnocchi to wrap slightly around your finger. See the Purple gnocchi ripieni with marsala shredded beef cheek and salsa verde (overleaf) for instructions on stuffing them.

GNUDI

1 For gnocchi's bare cousin gnudi, simply mix all but the semolina together well, flour your hands lightly, and roll into small balls. Toss well to coat in semolina and then refrigerate for 24 hours, loosely covered, before cooking.

NOTE Both gnocchi and gnudi should be transferred directly to floured surfaces or a sheet of baking paper as they are made, to avoid sticking.

Purple gnocchi ripieni with marsala shredded beef cheek and salsa verde

SERVES 8 | TOTAL TIME 1 HR 50 MINS

One of my favourite dishes that Ma still cooks for me is scaloppine. Scaloppine can be prepared so many different ways, with so many different flavours, that it's basically Italian for sliced meat in sauce. My ma's recipe though is an uncomplicated and delicious balance of thinly sliced and flour-dredged veal, cooked with bacon and marsala. While that's a perfect meal in itself, we love stuffing things into pasta, and so have adapted it to fill our gnocchi. We've served them here pan-fried, and with an old-fashioned boiled-egg salsa verde.

GNOCCHI

- 2 × quantities Gnocchi dough (page 25), made with a purple variety of potato
- 400 g (14 oz) beef cheek, cubed
- 2 tablespoons extra-virgin olive oil
- 80 g (2¾ oz) short-cut bacon, rind removed
- 4 garlic cloves, chopped
- 120 ml (4 fl oz) dry marsala
- 200 ml (7 fl oz) beef stock
- 60 g (2 oz/¼ cup) butter

SALSA VERDE

- 100 g (3½ oz) parsley, finely chopped
- 20 g (¾ oz) capers, rinsed
- 2 preserved anchovy fillets
- 2 garlic cloves, minced
- 1 tablespoon extra-virgin olive oil
- 1 hard-boiled egg, chopped
- juice of 1 lemon
- salt and freshly cracked black pepper, to taste

Prepare the gnocchi dough (see Gnocchi, gnudi: Tutorial, page 163) and refrigerate.

Brown the beef in the olive oil, uncovered in a pressure cooker, on a high heat for 2–3 minutes. Add the bacon and garlic, cooking for a further 2–3 minutes, or until it begins to brown. Deglaze with the marsala and allow it to evaporate before pouring in the stock and sealing the pressure cooker. If the stock does not cover the meat, add water as required. Cook on a low heat for 1 hour.

Depressurise, and use two forks to pull apart the beef. Raise the heat to medium and cook for 5–10 minutes, or until most of the liquid has been absorbed or evaporated. Remove from the heat and allow to cool.

To prepare the gnocchi, form the dough into large, walnut-sized balls, then flatten into discs. Place a small dollop of filling into the centre and then bring the edges up to meet, forming a filled ball. To form square shapes, press each into a square cookie cutter, against a flat work surface. Alternatively, gently flatten into discs, keeping the dough join centred underneath the gnocchi.

To cook the gnocchi, drop them into a large pot of lightly salted boiling water. They should be ready when they float, about 4–5 minutes. Scoop out and drain, patting dry to remove any remaining water.

Next, melt the butter in a frying pan over a medium heat. Fry the gnocchi in small batches, cooking until a light brown crust forms, about 4–5 minutes. Ensure that you turn them to brown each side.

Prepare the salsa verde by pounding together all the ingredients in a mortar and pestle, or blitzing in a blender until mostly smooth.

Serve the gnocchi with the salsa verde, and a fresh crack of pepper.

ON PASTA

Though this book doesn't feature them, use the same dough recipe (without the filling) to turn out regular unfilled gnocchi.

ON INGREDIENTS

For colour, we normally choose Purple Bliss or Midnight Pearl varieties of potato, but any of your favourite spuds will work in this versatile stuffed gnocchi format.

For a little extra crunch, retain the potato skins. Drizzle with a splash of olive oil, sprinkle with salt, and roast them in a 200°C (390°F) oven for 5–10 minutes until crispy.

Gnudi with asparagus and lemon

SERVES 4 | TOTAL TIME 30 MINS, PLUS 24 HRS

Gnudi are what happen when you pipe out your leftover ravioli filling and leave it to dry up for 24 hours. In the nicest possible way. They're fluffy and delicate, with an outer coating just firm enough to hold them together. This light and uncomplicated butter sauce adds just the right amount of flavour and silkiness without drowning out their subtlety. Aldo enjoys rolling these out 'just like pignolata'.

- 1 × quantity Gnudi dough (page 25)
- 100 g (3½ oz) butter
- 2 garlic cloves, lightly smashed
- 200 g (7 oz) asparagus, thinly slivered
- zest of ½ lemon
- cracked black pepper, to serve

Form the dough into gnudi (see Gnocchi, gnudi: Tutorial, page 163). Cover loosely and refrigerate for 24 hours. This will seal the soft filling within a firm crust and prevent them falling apart when cooked.

Melt the butter in a large frying pan over a medium heat, then add the garlic and asparagus. Increase the heat to medium–high and fry, stirring, until the asparagus begins to brown, about 4–5 minutes. Remove the garlic cloves.

Gently boil the gnudi for 2–3 minutes, until they float, then scoop directly into the frying pan; retain a little pasta water. Toss well and add enough of that pasta water to coat the gnudi well.

Serve with the lemon zest and a little cracked pepper.

ON PASTA

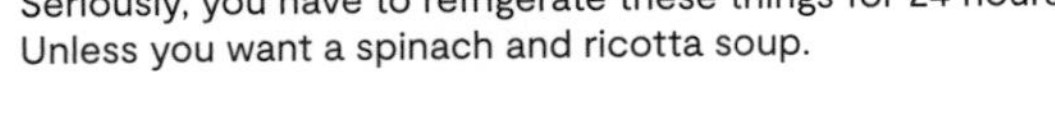

Seriously, you have to refrigerate these things for 24 hours. Unless you want a spinach and ricotta soup.

ON INGREDIENTS

If you find your grated zest a little too bitter, try peeling and chopping it with a knife instead to better avoid or more easily scrape off the white pith.

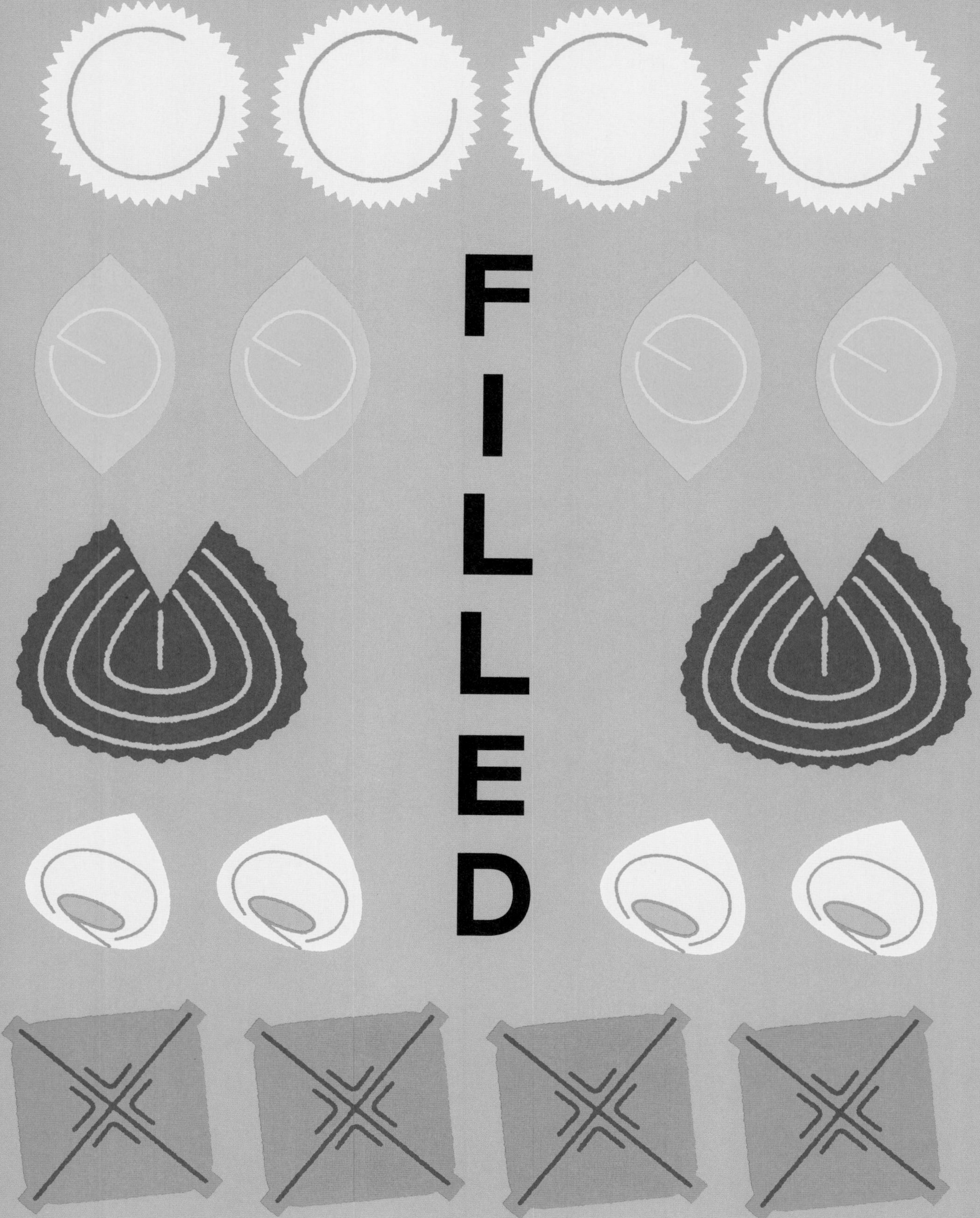
FILLED

There's something particularly irresistible about filled pasta, with their endless interplays of form and flavour, and such beauty in the design that brings these factors together. Although perhaps the most difficult type of pasta to craft, there's nothing that you can't master with a little know-how and practice. This chapter will guide you through our favourite filled pasta, beginning with the simpler stamped shapes of ravioli, anolini and sfoglia lorda, through to the folds of agnolotti del plin, fagottini, caramelle, balanzoni, tortelli, cappellacci, cappelletti and (Aldo's favourite) scarpinocc. You'll be plating up your own handmade masterpieces in no time.

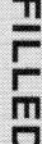

Ravioli

There are three main ways that we make our ravioli: with a mould, with a stamp and with little more than a pastry cutter.

To use a ravioli mould, roll your egg pasta dough into sheets of medium–thin thickness, about 1–1.5 mm (1/16 in). Traditionally, you should be able to read a newspaper through it, but Nonna always went thicker and so we do too. Everything's just a little coarser in the south.

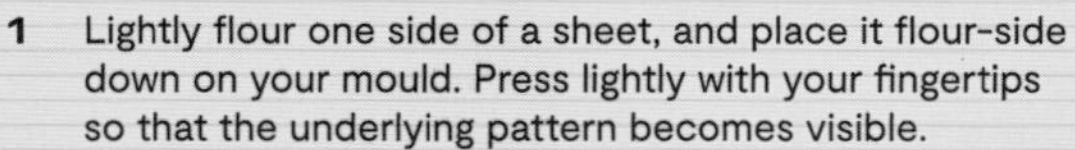

1 Lightly flour one side of a sheet, and place it flour-side down on your mould. Press lightly with your fingertips so that the underlying pattern becomes visible.

2 Pipe or spoon in your filling, and cover with another pasta sheet.

3 Lightly flour, and roll firmly with a pin (as shown in the next image). You should see the mould cutting through the dough, and any joined pieces separating. Turn the mould over and knock the ravioli free by gently tapping the mould on your work surface.

NOTE that larger moulds may require more than one sheet top and bottom to cover all depressions. Simply overlap the edges of two with a light brush of water in between the join.

If using a stamp, lay one sheet of pasta out flat and cover with dollops of filling sized and spaced appropriately for the stamp that you'll be using. Cover with another sheet, flour well, and stamp around the lumps. Don't feel limited by actual cutters – even the opening of a drinking glass will seal the pasta, and a slightly larger cookie cutter or large, sharp knife will cut it free.

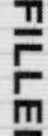

1 We sometimes also make tiny or odd-shaped ravioli with just a thin dowel and a pastry cutter. Prepare your filled sheets as you would for a stamp, but then use a dowel to firmly press grids around the filling.

2 Give it a wiggle and a roll to make sure that it's sealed properly, then trace the lines with your pastry cutter or a sharp knife to form into individual ravioli. Be especially careful to avoid trapping air, as this may cause the ravioli to pop when boiled.

1 Doppio ravioli are often made with this last method, leaving uncut one join between two separately filled halves. Either form like traditional ravioli, albeit with a centre divide, or more like agnolotti. For this latter method, pipe two fillings side-by-side on one half of a pasta rectangle, then fold the other half over them and seal around the filling, ensuring there's a divide down the middle.

2 Bring the narrower edges together over the centre divide, and pinch together. You can also pipe them along one continuous sheet of pasta, just make sure that when you cut the individual pieces out you don't accidentally sever the pairs.

Spinach and ricotta ravioli with sugo and meatballs

SERVES 4 | TOTAL TIME 5 HRS

These days I make all kinds of pasta with all kinds of dough, but when I was a kid there were only a few types that ever made it to the table. Don't get me wrong, we enjoyed a little extra variety in the occasional packet pasta – secretly but unanimously excited as my nonna apologised for the rigatoni she was opening – but when we did it ourselves, our repertoire was deliberately and appropriately limited. We made spinach and ricotta ravioli, always with spinach dough, and we made spinach fettuccine with the leftovers. On occasion we'd roll out some plain dough lasagne, sometimes gnocchi, but for the most part we were a green pasta family. To this day, the only dough that truly tastes 'right' to me is freshly made spinach.

As the oldest grandchild, I'd mostly graduated from Nonna's scuola di cucina (or at least been finally expelled) by the time my brother and cousins arrived to bolster the workforce. But in the years before school, and on the weekends until they could passably turn a pasta handle, I would stand for hours beside my nonna churning out ludicrous amounts of pasta for the extended family, usually to last months at a time. And months at a time, in an Italian family, equates to a significant amount of pasta. I don't mean to claim any sort of mystical pasta knowledge gleaned from a childhood spent staring into pasta sheets, but it did teach me how to cook by taste and feel. Nonna's 'recipes' were along the lines of 'you put flour in a bowl and mix in eggs'. And it certainly taught me how to make spinach and ricotta ravioli. In many ways, pasta for me started from and continues with this recipe, typically served with Nonna's sugo, meatballs on the side.

1 × quantity Spinach dough (page 24)

FILLING

- 400 g (14 oz) fresh ricotta
- 100 g (3½ oz/2 cups) fresh baby spinach leaves, blanched, thoroughly drained and chopped (after blanching, this will reduce to around 50 g/1¾ oz/1 cup, so substitute accordingly if using frozen spinach)
- 1 egg
- 25 g (1 oz) pecorino Romano, grated, or similar hard cheese, plus extra to serve
- salt and freshly cracked black pepper, to season

SUGO

- ½ onion, diced
- ½ garlic bulb, minced
- 100 ml (3½ fl oz) extra-virgin olive oil, or more if you want to really treat yourself
- 1 small handful of basil
- 700 ml (23½ fl oz) passata (puréed tomatoes)
- ½ teaspoon sugar
- salt and freshly cracked black pepper, to taste

MEATBALLS

- 250 g (9 oz) minced (ground) pork
- 250 g (9 oz) minced (ground) veal or beef
- 45 g (1½ oz) breadcrumbs, or one large slice of bread soaked in milk and squeezed
- 25 g (1 oz) pecorino Romano, grated
- 1 egg
- 1 small handful of parsley, finely chopped

Mix all the filling ingredients together and transfer to a piping bag fitted with a medium round tip. You can easily use a bag without the tip, or even substitute with a teaspoon, but I find these methods less efficient when producing large batches of filled pasta.

Form the pasta dough into sheets of around 1 mm (1⁄16 in) thickness (see Handmade pasta: Tutorial, page 33), then use the filling to make ravioli (see Ravioli: Tutorial, page 172). We've used a large grid mould for these.

ON PASTA

Most pasta will work with this sugo, even those stuffed with meat (as the meatballs can be served separately, leaving a versatile tomato sauce). My better half declares it 'the world's best sugo', and she's not one for superlative munificence.

ON INGREDIENTS

It's all in the soffritto. Take it slowly, stir it continuously, and nurse it to sweaty perfection. The rest will take care of itself.

To make the sugo, to a large cold pot, add the onion and half of the minced garlic with the olive oil. Set over a very low heat and stir gently but continuously for 25–30 minutes until the onion is sweaty and translucent. Do not let it brown. It can help to occasionally turn the heat off altogether and let it sit for a few minutes before continuing.

Bruise the basil in your hand then add to the pot, frying gently for 2–3 minutes. Pour in the passata, then half-fill the bottle with water. Slosh it around to collect any remaining tomato, then add to the pot. Season the sauce with the sugar and a good pinch of salt, stir, then increase the heat to medium.

For the meatballs, place the pork and beef mince in a large bowl with the breadcrumbs, grated cheese, egg, the remaining minced garlic (from the sugo), parsley and a seasoning of salt and pepper. Knead together with your hands, allowing the mix to squeeze through your fingers. Break off plum-sized balls, then roll, turn and squeeze them into smooth meatballs using your palms. Transfer to a baking tray lined with baking paper and refrigerate until required.

Once the sauce is at a gentle boil, drop the raw meatballs straight in. Try to avoid stirring with a wooden spoon until they've firmed up; instead, occasionally shuffle the pot gently by the handles for the first few minutes. Set over a low heat and cook for at least 3.5 hours, with the lid slightly ajar. We prop it open with the handle of a wooden spoon. Stir regularly, keeping an eye on the liquid levels and making sure that it doesn't catch. If it becomes too dry, top it up with water and lower the heat further. You'll know that it's ready once the sugo has turned a dark red with oily puddles on top.

To cook the ravioli, drop them into lightly salted and vigorously boiling water; cook until still firm but with no raw white dough visible when cut into, about 4–5 minutes. Lift the meatballs out of the pot, to be served separately, and stir the ravioli directly into the sauce. Serve with some extra grated pecorino.

Doppio ravioli of roasted pumpkin and chestnut with spun balsamic sugar

SERVES 4 | TOTAL TIME 1 HR 45 MINS

Doppio ravioli are a bit of an indulgence. They're not an every-weekend sort of pasta, but they do make for an interesting way to distinctly pair complementary flavours. One of our favourite combinations is roasted potato and capsicum (bell pepper), but pumpkin (squash) and chestnut are mellow, cosy alternatives.

We first dreamed up our spun balsamic sugar as a way of doing something playfully messy, a bit fancy, and not overpoweringly sweet despite its main ingredient being sugar. The balsamic cuts through the sugar and adds a little bit of acid around the edges of every mouthful. With some care for hot bits and pieces, our simple method of building these wispy nests is a tried and tested toddler-pleaser. And I challenge you to resist taking a selfie with one on your head.

- 120 g (4½ oz) raw chestnuts
- 100 g (3½ oz) ricotta
- 20 g (¾ oz) taleggio
- 20 g (¾ oz) Parmigiano Reggiano, grated
- salt and freshly cracked black pepper, to taste
- 200 g (7 oz) pumpkin (squash), chopped into large cubes
- 20 cherry or baby roma (plum) tomatoes
- 1 small rosemary sprig
- 2 tablespoons extra-virgin olive oil
- 1 garlic bulb, with the top 1 cm (½ in) cut off
- 1 × quantity Whole egg and egg yolk dough (page 19)
- 100 g (3½ oz) caster (superfine) sugar
- 1 tablespoon balsamic vinegar
- 5 g (⅛ oz) glucose

Preheat the oven to 200°C (390°F). Use a sharp knife to score each of the chestnuts (this will help when it comes time to peel them), then add them to a pot of cold water. Bring to the boil and cook for 25–30 minutes until a knife can be easily slid into the flesh.

Drain the chestnuts and remove the skins, then mash together with 80 g (2¾ oz) of the ricotta, the taleggio and Parmigiano Reggiano, seasoning to taste. Load into a piping bag.

Toss the pumpkin, tomatoes and rosemary together with 1 tablespoon of the olive oil, season and roast with the garlic in the oven. Remove the garlic and tomatoes after 15–20 minutes (once the tomato skins begin to blister and brown slightly), and the pumpkin after 30 minutes. Allow the pumpkin to cool, then discard the skin.

Squeeze the garlic out of the bulb and mash together with the pumpkin and remaining ricotta. Season to taste then load into another piping bag.

Roll your pasta dough out into sheets of approximately 1 mm (1⁄16 in) thickness (see Handmade pasta: Tutorial, page 33), cut into rectangles of around sheet width – 12–14 × 7–8 cm (4¾–5½ × 2¾–3¼ in) – and then use the two fillings to make doppio ravioli (see Ravioli: Tutorial, page 172). To do this, pipe a thumb-sized dollop of each filling side-by-side running lengthways down the centre of the rectangle with a finger's gap in between them. Fold over as if making agnolotti and seal around the filling, ensuring there's a divide down the middle. If desired, cut a zigzag along the long edge using a pastry cutter. Bring the narrower edges together over the centre divide, and pinch together to complete. Alternatively, pipe a line of each filling onto a square of dough, covering with another sheet, then seal and cut to shape.

ON PASTA

This is a great opportunity to pair your own favourite flavours. We love a potato-based filling in one and roasted capsicum (bell pepper) in the other.

ON INGREDIENTS

Yes, the quantities of spun sugar ingredients allow for the inevitable mess that you will make while refining your technique and perfecting that first nest.

To make the spun balsamic sugar, heat the sugar, 3 teaspoons water, balsamic vinegar and glucose in a pan. Technically, you're aiming for 140–150°C (285–300°F), but I never bother with a thermometer. Instead, let it thicken until it briefly holds its place when you drag a spatula through it. Then remove from the heat and allow to cool until long delicate wisps form as it runs off the spatula.

Prepare a small cake tin or similar round object by wrapping it in baking paper (or silicone), fastening it in place with sticky tape and/or an elastic band. Next, lay a heavy wooden spoon on its side, on a bench, with the handle hanging over the edge and paper towel underneath. Drizzle the syrup along the handle so that tendrils of syrup stretch down towards the ground. Roll the tendrils around the cake tin until you're happy with your nest. Note that the sugar will eventually cool to the point of becoming brittle, and anything left in the pan will solidify. If this happens, simply break off the piece that you're wrapping, and return the pan to the heat to re-melt before continuing.

Boil the pasta in a large pot of salted water for 4–5 minutes, test for doneness, then drain. Toss with the remaining olive oil and a little cracked pepper, and serve with the roasted cherry tomatoes inside the balsamic nest. Note that you should serve immediately after plating, as the nest will begin to dissolve.

Anolini, sfoglia lorda

Very similar to ravioli (see page 172), anolini and sfoglia lorda are essentially made by spreading, rather than dolloping, filling between two sheets of pasta.

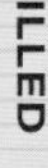

1 Take a sheet of any egg dough (see page 18). Roll to a thickness of 1–2 mm ($^{1}/_{16}$–$^{1}/_{8}$ in) and evenly coat it with a thin layer of pasta filling. A spatula will help.

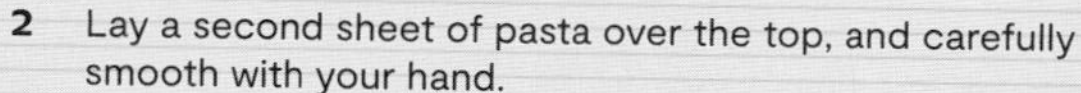

2 Lay a second sheet of pasta over the top, and carefully smooth with your hand.

3 To make anolini, use any small, round cutter to stamp out the individual pasta. You can use a regular round ravioli stamp, or even large piping bag tips.

1 For sfoglia lorda, use a pastry cutter to cut into a grid of squares.

NOTE Both of these pasta shapes benefit from smoother fillings that won't interfere with the seal produced by the cutter.

Walnut and chicory anolini with mushroom broth

SERVES 4 | TOTAL TIME 1 HR 40 MINS

Does stuffed pasta get any easier than anolini? Simply spread your filling between two sheets and stamp it into circles. This subtly flavoured anolini in a broth is really a whatever-leftovers-you've-got kind of thing, and when we first made it that meant a little chicory (endive) and a handful of pantry staples.

We like to serve a mix of greens alongside our pasta (our usual trio is broccoli, zucchini/courgette and beans), but for a special treat we add in a side of balsamic caramelised radicchio and blanch and fry some chicory with garlic. This filling uses some of that chicory, with otherwise uncooked ingredients, and our quick broth is bolstered by dried porcini and an old cheese rind.

1 × quantity Whole egg and egg yolk dough (page 19)

FILLING

- 60 g (2 oz) chicory (endive)
- 60 g (2 oz) dry breadcrumbs
- 60 g (2 oz/½ cup) walnuts, chopped
- 1 tablespoon full-cream (whole) milk
- 1 garlic clove
- big squeeze of lemon juice
- pinch of salt

BROTH

- ½ carrot, roughly chopped
- ½ onion, roughly chopped
- 2 garlic cloves, smashed
- 1 tablespoon extra-virgin olive oil
- 200 g (7 oz) fresh mushrooms, roughly chopped
- 20 g (¾ oz) dried porcini mushrooms
- large chunk of Parmigiano Reggiano rind
- 2 sage leaves
- 1 bay leaf
- salt and freshly cracked black pepper, to taste

For the filling, begin by boiling the chicory in a large pot of salted water for 15 minutes. Drain, allow to cool, then chop finely. Soak the breadcrumbs and walnuts in the milk mixed with 40 ml (1¼ fl oz) water for 10–15 minutes, then blend together with the chicory, garlic and lemon juice; season to taste with a pinch of salt. Add a little more water if it's not at a spreadable consistency.

Roll the pasta dough out into sheets of approximately 1–2 mm (1⁄16–⅛ in) thickness (see Handmade pasta: Tutorial, page 33), spread the filling between paired sheets, and stamp out anolini (see Anolini, sfoglia lorda: Tutorial, page 178).

In a large pot, sauté the carrot, onion and garlic in the olive oil for 5–6 minutes, or until the vegetables begin to brown. Add the mushrooms, cheese rind, herbs and 1.5 litres (51 fl oz/6 cups) water; reduce the heat to low and cook for 35–40 minutes. Strain well, discarding the solids, then return the broth to the pot and reduce for another 10–15 minutes. Season to taste.

Boil the anolini in a large pot of salted water for 3–4 minutes, until done, then drain and serve with the broth.

ON PASTA

The smoother and thinner your filling, the less chance that your pasta will break open during cooking. These anolini are well-substituted by sfoglia lorda (see page 178) or any small variety of unfilled pasta.

ON INGREDIENTS

For a traditionally cheap and common ingredient, chicory (endive) can be hard to track down. Substitute with a leafier green, like spinach, noting that it will only need a few minutes on the boil.

Pistachio and ricotta sfoglia lorda in broccoli soup

SERVES 4 | TOTAL TIME 1 HR 15 MINS

Yes, stuffed pasta does get easier than anolini (see page 178). Sfoglia lorda, or spoja lorda, is another marvel of pasta design for its elegant simplicity. Spread your filling between two sheets of pasta and slice it into squares with a pastry cutter. By keeping the filling smooth and spreading it thinly, the cutter seals and divides all at once, producing quick little parcels similar to flat ravioli.

Like anolini, this versatile shape is suited to broths and sauces alike. We've served it in an easy broth of broccoli and zucchini (courgette), but it works just as well in a nice sugo.

1 × quantity Whole egg dough (page 18)

SOUP

- 400 g (14 oz) broccoli, chopped into small pieces
- 200 g (7 oz) zucchini (courgette), diced
- 4 garlic cloves, roughly chopped
- 2 litres (68 fl oz/8 cups) vegetable stock
- squeeze of lemon juice
- salt and freshly cracked black pepper, to taste

FILLING

- 60 g (2 oz) pistachios, shelled and toasted
- 30 ml (1 fl oz) full-cream (whole) milk
- 160 g (5½ oz/⅔ cup) ricotta
- 20 g (¾ oz) Parmigiano Reggiano, finely grated
- 1 egg
- salt and freshly cracked black pepper

Add all the soup ingredients to a large pot and bring to the boil over a high heat. Drop to a low heat, cover and cook for 35 minutes. Mash gently, partially breaking up the vegetables, then season to taste.

To make the pasta filling, soak the pistachios in the milk for 10–15 minutes, then drain and use a mortar and pestle to grind to a paste. Mix with the ricotta, Parmigiano Reggiano and egg. Season well.

Roll the pasta dough out into 1–2 mm (1⁄16–⅛ in) thick sheets (see Handmade pasta: Tutorial, page 33), then spread the filling evenly between them, forming into sfoglia lorda (see Anolini, sfoglia lorda: Tutorial, page 178).

Bring the soup to the boil, drop the pasta in and cook for 3–4 minutes, checking for doneness.

ON PASTA

Any small, unfilled pasta works well in soup, or even scrappy maltagliati offcuts.

ON INGREDIENTS

Whenever you're making a predominantly ricotta filling like this, resist the temptation to hit it with a high-speed stick blender or food processor. Definitely blitz any other filling ingredients together, but when it comes to the ricotta, stir it through to avoid it becoming a sudden runny mess.

TUTORIAL

Agnolotti del plin

These little pillows of pasta are formed with a fold, a pinch, and a cut, making them an elegant and ever-so-satisfying shape to craft.

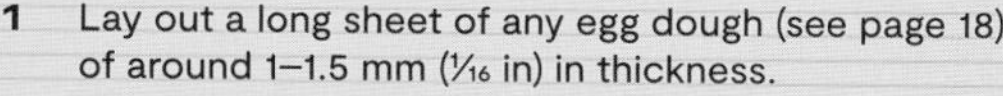

1 Lay out a long sheet of any egg dough (see page 18) of around 1–1.5 mm (1/16 in) in thickness.

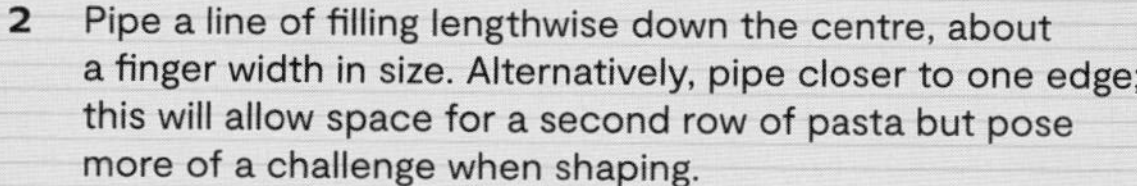

2 Pipe a line of filling lengthwise down the centre, about a finger width in size. Alternatively, pipe closer to one edge; this will allow space for a second row of pasta but pose more of a challenge when shaping.

3 Pick up and fold one long edge over the filling. Press down lightly with your fingers where the dough overlaps, following the length of the filling, and removing any trapped air. Seal each end.

4 Leaving around one finger's width of flat dough beside the filling, use a pastry cutter to trim the excess unfilled dough. You should now have what looks like a giant filled pappardelle, sealed on one side.

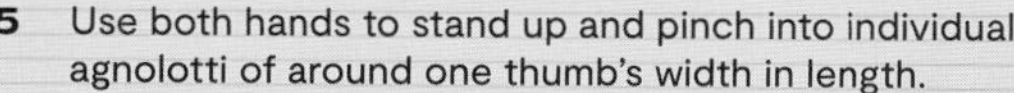

5 Use both hands to stand up and pinch into individual agnolotti of around one thumb's width in length.

6 Finally, use a pastry cutter to cut across the channels that you've just pinched, working from the unbroken side to where you first overlapped the dough. As you cut, the pasta will fold over itself forming its final shape. You may need to use your free hand to guide each piece as it topples over and seals.

Agnolotti del plin with tomato consommé

SERVES 4 | TOTAL TIME 1 HR 35 MINS

A tomato consommé is an excellent way of cramming in a heap of tomatoey flavour without the richness that you get from using whole tomatoes. As sacrilegious as it feels to be removing all that flesh, a thin, refined consommé can pair wonderfully with a bold pasta filling.

Agnolotti del plin are typically filled with an even punchier combination of meats than we've opted for here. A Piedmontese specialty (named for the local word for 'pinch'), you'll usually find them filled with mixed roasted meats, making it a great way to use up dinner leftovers in a way that honours their origins. We blend it all up so that it can be piped in one long strip, but for a chunkier filling, simply line up a row of generous dollops, allowing room for a clean seal.

1 × quantity Whole egg and egg yolk dough (page 19)

FILLING

- 60 g (2 oz) mortadella, finely chopped
- 120 g (4½ oz) minced (ground) beef
- 120 g (4½ oz) minced (ground) pork
- 2 tablespoons extra-virgin olive oil
- 80 g (2¾ oz) ricotta
- 40 g (1½ oz) frozen spinach, defrosted, drained and finely chopped
- 1 egg

CONSOMMÉ

- 1 onion, coarsely chopped
- 2 garlic cloves, coarsely chopped
- 2 tablespoons extra-virgin olive oil
- 2 kg (4 lb 6 oz) fresh tomatoes, coarsely blended
- 1 small handful of parsley leaves
- 1 small handful of basil leaves
- salt and freshly cracked black pepper, to taste
- 8 egg whites, whisked

To make the pasta filling, fry the mortadella, beef and pork mince in the oil in a large frying pan over a high heat until crispy, 5–8 minutes. Remove from the heat and, once cool, blend into a paste with the other filling ingredients. Load into a piping bag with a medium round tip.

Roll the pasta dough into sheets of around 1.5 mm (1⁄16 in) thickness (see Handmade pasta: Tutorial, page 33), then use the filling to form agnolotti del plin (see Agnolotti del plin: Tutorial, page 184).

For the consommé, gently sauté the onion and garlic in the oil in a large pot for 15 minutes, or until soft; stir regularly to avoid browning. Add the tomato and herbs, season well, and then cook, uncovered, for another 15–20 minutes.

Strain the mixture, returning the liquid to the pot, and then bring it to a gentle boil before adding the egg whites. Whisk a few times, then allow the whites to form a layer on top of the liquid. Break a gap in the centre to allow bubbles to escape, then cook undisturbed for 15 minutes. The egg whites will help to further clarify the consommé.

Remove from the heat and carefully lift off the egg whites. Strain well through a fine piece of muslin (cheesecloth), or similar.

Cook the pasta in a large pot of salted water for 4–5 minutes, or until done, then serve in the consommé.

ON PASTA

We love this shape in broth because it captures a little liquid in its envelope-like fold. You'll get a similar effect with tortellini. For the filling, with a lighter broth like this, you'll probably want to keep it on the punchier side.

ON INGREDIENTS

Use fresh, vine-ripened tomatoes for the fullest flavour.

Smoky nettle agnolotti del plin with toasted chilli oil

SERVES 4 | TOTAL TIME 1 HR

I can just imagine the incredulous grin on the face of the owner of the overgrown garden from which my greengrocer used to source my nettles. Getting paid to weed their own backyard. Presumably, I could only ever purchase by the carton because it would otherwise fail to produce a sufficient dent in their workload, and would hardly be worth donning the necessary chain mail. I've since moved to more nettle-riddled lands, and taken to clearing the yards of bewildered neighbours instead.

Despite or perhaps due to being a prickly nuisance, nettles have been used in Italian cooking for a very long time, and make an exceptionally vibrant and interesting substitution for spinach in green pasta dough. Just make sure that you choose the smaller top leaves, picked well before the plants start flowering (the most tender foliage) and boil it all up for 2–3 minutes before handling any further, to neutralise the sting.

- 60 ml (2 fl oz/¼ cup) extra-virgin olive oil
- 20 g (¾ oz) dried red chilli flakes
- 1 × quantity Nettle dough (page 24), made with ½ teaspoon liquid smoke stirred in with the eggs
- grated hard cheese, to serve

FILLING

- 60 g (2 oz/½ cup) roasted walnuts, chopped
- 120 g (4½ oz) mascarpone
- 80 g (2¾ oz) ash-coated chèvre
- 20 g (¾ oz) panko breadcrumbs
- 1 egg
- salt and freshly cracked black pepper, to taste

Warm the oil in a small pot over a medium heat until hot and shimmering, 3–4 minutes (or, more accurately, to a temperature of around 180°C/360°F). Place the chilli in a small heatproof bowl and pour the hot oil over the top. The chilli should toast without burning. Allow to infuse for 20–30 minutes.

To prepare the pasta filling, grind the walnuts to a paste using a mortar and pestle, then stir together with the mascarpone, chèvre, breadcrumbs and egg. Season to taste and load into a piping bag with a medium round tip.

Roll the dough out into sheets of about 1 mm (1/16 in) thickness (see Handmade pasta: Tutorial, page 33), then use the filling to form agnolotti del plin (see Agnolotti del plin: Tutorial, page 184).

Boil the pasta in a large pot of salted water until done, about 4–5 minutes. Scoop a few ladles of the pasta water into a large mixing bowl and vigorously whisk in the chilli oil until it emulsifies into a smooth sauce. Use a slotted spoon to toss the pasta in straight from the pot and stir to combine. Serve with a freshly grated hard cheese and cracked black pepper.

ON PASTA

If you'd like a green dough that's not made with nettles, try spinach (see page 23). Note though that nettles give this pasta a very particular, striking green that you won't be able to replicate without a substantially higher ratio of spinach. Any pasta will substitute in well with a toasted chilli oil like this.

ON INGREDIENTS

As noted in the dough recipe, make sure that you boil your nettle leaves for a few minutes before cooking with them. This will neutralise the sting. Until you've done so, handle with rubber gloves.

TUTORIAL

Fagottini

A geometric delight, unlike any other pasta shape out there. Fagottini are perfect boiled, fried, in sauce, or in broth.

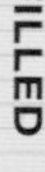

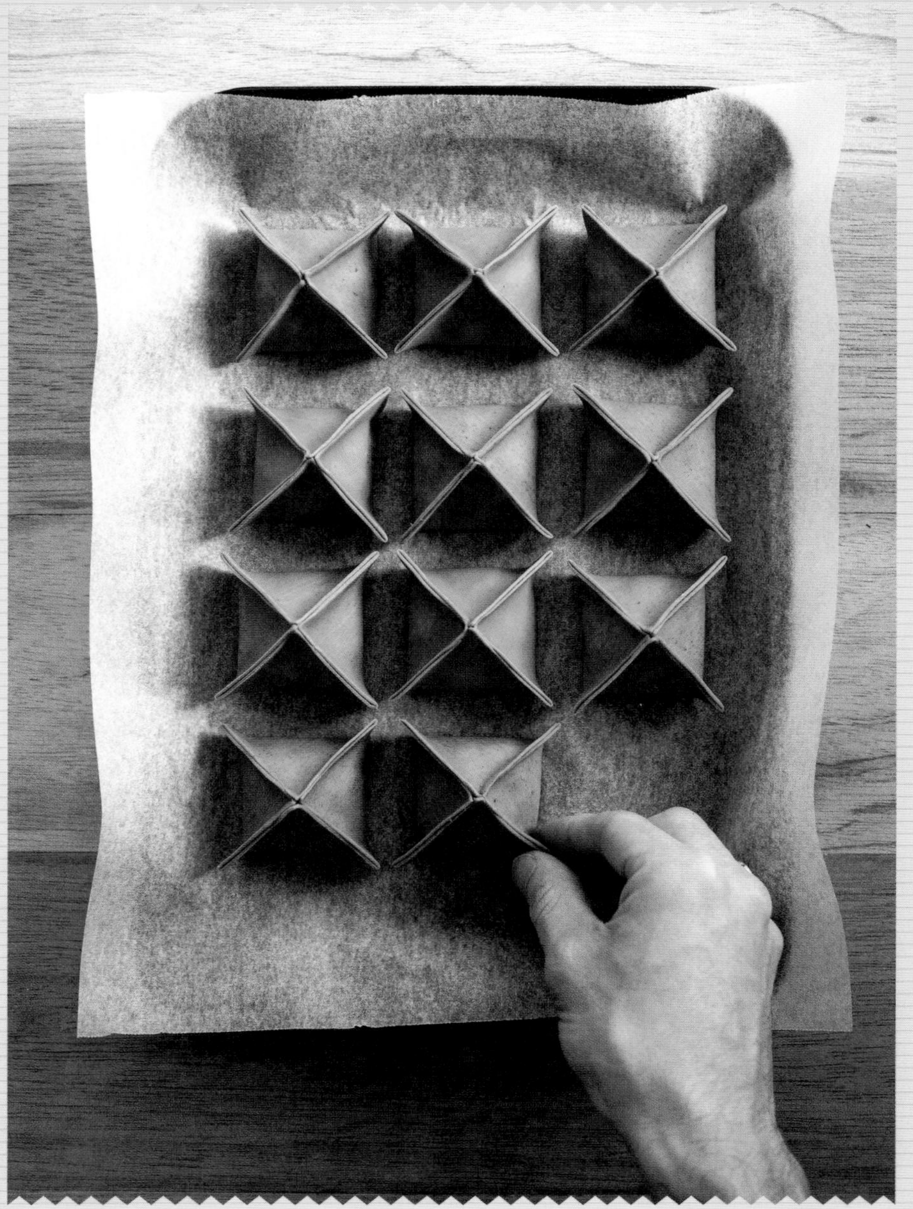

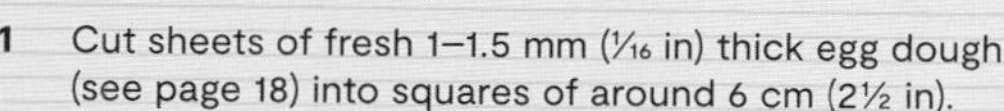

1 Cut sheets of fresh 1–1.5 mm (1/16 in) thick egg dough (see page 18) into squares of around 6 cm (2½ in).

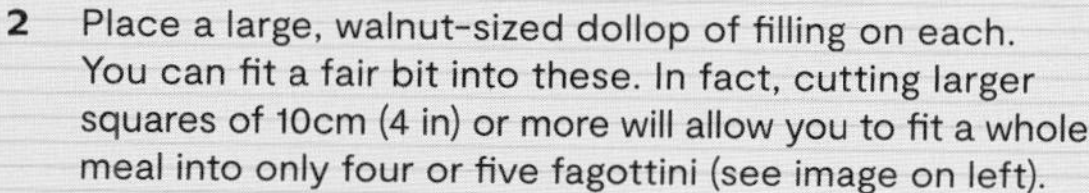

2 Place a large, walnut-sized dollop of filling on each. You can fit a fair bit into these. In fact, cutting larger squares of 10cm (4 in) or more will allow you to fit a whole meal into only four or five fagottini (see image on left).

3 Bring the corners together in pairs, pinching the very tips together, but leaving the edges open. It should be rectangular in shape, with openings on the ends and above the filling.

4 With the corners still pinched between your fingers, bring them into the centre above the filling and press together to form a pyramid. Seal the open edges.

NOTE A related shape that's worth a shot is sacchettoni. Simply gather the dough up and squeeze it together just above the filling, forming a little moneybag. This shape is possible with both square and round base shapes. Just be sure to pinch that centre together well to avoid undercooked dough later on.

Four cheese and white bean fagottini with pressure-cooker bone broth

SERVES 4 | TOTAL TIME 4 HRS 40 MINS, PLUS OVERNIGHT

If you want to light a fire in the pasta world, just ask someone what these little guys are called. Even the eternal debate over fettuccine and tagliatelle is easier to settle than this one. Manti, fagottini, ravioli, cofanetti, lanterne. Unlike tagliatelle, fagottini does not exist stubbornly and indelibly cast in solid gold within the Bologna Chamber of Commerce, elevated beyond any dispute as to its origins or dimension. True story: 1 mm by 7 mm, before cooking. Still doesn't explain fettuccine, but it's fine, everybody just be cool about pasta.

Fagottini are a unique shape, easy to make, and delicious to eat. Drawing inspiration from the good old Bolognesi and their penchant for tortellini in brodo, we often serve them in broth. This pressure-cooker broth is, in fact, one of our very favourite recipes, endlessly tinkered with, and eternally stashed throughout the freezer. Plate it all up beautifully, and then promptly bury it under a mountain of cheese.

1 × quantity Whole egg dough (page 18)

BONE BROTH

- 800 g (1 lb 12 oz) beef bones
- 2 celery stalks, chopped
- 1 carrot, chopped
- 1 onion, chopped
- 6 garlic cloves, peeled and squashed
- 2 tablespoons extra-virgin olive oil
- 1 handful of thyme sprigs
- 1 handful of rosemary sprigs
- 1 handful of parsley, chopped
- 3–4 bay leaves
- 2 teaspoons black peppercorns
- 2 tablespoons apple-cider vinegar
- 2 teaspoons salt

FILLING

- 120 g (4½ oz) ricotta
- 35 g (1¼ oz) Grana Padano cheese, grated
- 35 g (1¼ oz) pecorino Romano cheese, grated, plus extra to serve
- 30 g (1 oz) gorgonzola cheese
- 80 g (2¾ oz) white beans, rinsed and puréed
- 1 egg
- 2 parsley sprigs, finely chopped
- freshly cracked black pepper, to taste

Preheat the oven to 200°C (390°F). Begin the broth by spreading the bones on a baking tray and roasting for 20 minutes.

Add the celery, carrot, onion and garlic to the pressure cooker with the olive oil. Sauté over a low heat, stirring, until the onion begins to soften and becomes transparent. Stir in the thyme, rosemary, parsley, bay leaves and peppercorns before raising the heat to medium and sautéing for a further 2–3 minutes, stirring.

Add the bones, vinegar and salt, and pour in enough water to just cover the bones. Note that if you're scaling this recipe up, your liquid level should be no higher than two-thirds of the pot. Seal the pressure cooker, raise the heat to high, then return it to low heat to cook for 3 hours.

Turn off the heat and allow the cooker to cool for half an hour before depressurising. If your pressure cooker allows it, step down through the pressure settings rather than immediately opening the steam valve. This broth will be very hot and may blast out of the pressure valve if depressurised too soon.

Once it has cooled enough to handle, strain the broth through a colander to remove the large chunks of veggies, bones and meat. Consider picking off and keeping the meat – it can make a great pasta filling or be quickly thrown into a stir-fry.

Pour the broth through a piece of muslin (cheesecloth) to remove finer impurities, and transfer to containers/bowls to cool. Once cool enough to refrigerate, cover and leave in the fridge overnight; this will cause the fat to solidify on the surface and make it much easier to remove from the broth.

Use a slotted spoon or similar to remove the fat solids from the surface; you may choose to keep this as a cooking fat, otherwise discard. The final broth should have a smooth, jelly-like consistency.

Transfer to storage containers until ready to use. It can be portioned and frozen, and when eaten either used as is or diluted with water to stretch further.

To make the fagottini filling, mix the cheeses together with the white beans, egg, parsley and seasoning; transfer to a piping bag with a medium round tip.

Roll the pasta dough into sheets of around 1 mm (1/16 in) thickness (see Handmade pasta: Tutorial, page 33), then cut into squares of approximately 6 cm (2½ in). Pipe a large, grape-sized dollop of filling into the centre of each square and form into fagottini (see Fagottini: Tutorial, page 190).

Drop the pasta into a large pot of salted boiling water and cook for 4–5 minutes, or until done. Serve the fagottini in bowls, with hot broth ladled over the top and a generous grating of cheese.

ON PASTA

You can stuff more into these little things than most filled pasta shapes, so don't hold back. Any other filled pasta is a fine substitute, and you can't go wrong stuffing them with meat either.

ON INGREDIENTS

Any mix of beef, lamb and pork bones works well. Just make sure that they're all fully submerged and don't fill that pressure cooker beyond two-thirds.

Pizzaiola fagottini potstickers with roasted green chilli

SERVES 4 | TOTAL TIME 1 HR 15 MINS

For all the talk of my nonna, and the pasta-making that she gifted to me, it was my ma who truly taught me how to cook. She always invited me to be by her side in the kitchen, let me help where I could, and showed me how good ingredients became good food. As I grew older, I also learned from her the other side of cooking: making the best from what you have, in whatever time you've got. She remains a master of both delicious, nutritious food, and preparing it with maximum efficiency. Watching her in the kitchen, she appears to move slowly (if at all), but feasts materialise around her with supernatural speed. More than anyone else credited in this book, I owe my ma for every little kitchen success I've ever had in life.

A dish that my brother and I both loved and fondly recall her cooking is pizzaiola. It's a quick steak meal that Ma would pluck together seemingly out of thin air in the time that it took one of us to pick a fight with the other, resolve it, and get changed out of our school clothes. For this recipe, we cooked Ma's good old pizzaiola and stuffed it into fagottini. Cooked as potstickers and served with a simple chilli sauce, it's a fun little take on a childhood favourite. For extra authenticity and danger, roast the chillies as Nonna would on the open flame of a semi-deconstructed gas burner.

1 × quantity Whole egg dough (page 18)

80 ml (2½ fl oz/⅓ cup) extra-virgin olive oil

FILLING

300 g (10½ oz) minced (ground) beef

2 garlic cloves, minced

80 ml (2½ fl oz/⅓ cup) extra-virgin olive oil

100 ml (3½ fl oz) white wine

200 g (7 oz) crushed tomatoes

40 g (1½ oz) green olives

1 teaspoon dried oregano

salt and freshly cracked black pepper, to taste

ROASTED GREEN CHILLI SAUCE

80 g (2¾ oz) fresh long green chillies, whole

1 small handful of parsley, finely chopped

1 tablespoon extra-virgin olive oil

1 tablespoon red-wine vinegar

1 garlic clove, finely chopped

splash of garum

salt and freshly cracked black pepper, to taste

pink peppercorns, lightly crushed, to serve

Fry the beef mince and garlic in the olive oil in a large frying pan over a medium–high heat, stirring, for 6–8 minutes, until brown and beginning to crisp.

Add the white wine and allow it to cook off before adding the tomatoes, olives and oregano; season to taste. Continue to cook uncovered until it has thickened into a spoonable consistency, about 10–15 minutes.

Prepare the green chilli sauce by first roasting the chillies over an open flame for 3–4 minutes until they're lightly scorched and soft. To easily remove the skins, seal the roasted chillies in an airtight container for 10 minutes before peeling. Blend coarsely with the parsley, olive oil, red-wine vinegar, garlic and garum. Season to taste.

Next, roll the pasta dough out into sheets of 1.5 mm (1/16 in) thickness (see Handmade pasta: Tutorial, page 33) and cut into large squares of 10 cm (4 in) across. Fill each with a large dollop of the meat mixture and form into fagottini (see Fagottini: Tutorial, page 190).

Fry the pasta in batches of around 7–8, using 2 tablespoons of olive oil at a time, in a medium-hot pan until the undersides are golden brown and crispy. Add 120 ml (4 fl oz) water, cover and cook for 3–4 minutes until all of the water has been absorbed or evaporated and the pasta is firm but done.

Serve with the roasted green chilli sauce and a scattering of pink peppercorns.

ON PASTA

I'm not going to try and stop you frying up any other filled pasta, but fagottini are uniquely perfect as potstickers. Their flat base gets deliciously and uniformly crispy, and the central sealed point above acts like a little chimney. If you want to try your hand at cooking any other filled pasta this way, I recommend making them big pieces.

ON INGREDIENTS

Those chillies can, of course, be roasted on a barbecue or even on a high heat in the oven. And if you want the flavour but not the heat, substitute with green capsicum (bell pepper).

On the future

Or, Tomato Day. Throughout a childhood of being asked whether we made tomato sauce, our little band of cousins became pretty good at joking summaries of days spent sitting around on milk crates with paring knives, Nonna ordering everyone about in her little knotted handkerchief hat. It's hilarious and we're proud of it, but it's also easier than trying to express what it actually means to us. Particularly now that we've all grown up and set off on our own lives.

For me at least, those were times of such intense happiness and belonging that rarely a day goes by without me wishing I could live even one of those moments again. There was my bisnonna ('Big Nonna', or great-grandmother) in charge of the whole thing with my nonna second-in-command, my ma and her brother and sister, all of us cousins, and occasionally a slightly baffled outsider. There was scheming with a carefully chosen farmer entrusted with the task of growing our family tomatoes, and the days leading up to the big event where Nonna would keep the tomatoes spread across a bed sheet on her garage floor to finish ripening. A 5 am start, endless coffee and regimented break times, freshly picked basil leaves taken straight from the garden to drop into each bottle, that perfect smell of salted tomatoes alongside engine grease and firewood. And, of course, enough dark brown beer bottles, re-collected as they were used over the previous year, to fill and distribute to the whole family for another twelve months. Every time any of us plucked one of those bottles out of its cool, dark hiding spot to cook with, we were immediately taken back to that day in Nonna's garage.

LEFT Aldo inspecting the tomatoes

ABOVE Salt being added to draw out excess water. Once the seeds are removed, the tomatoes are salted and suspended in cloth to drain before being wrung out and fed into the machine. After a few passes, the purée is bottled, capped and boiled.

'Tomato Day, after all those years, was not just about the tomatoes ...'

Cutting up tomatoes with my cousin Danica, Aldo and wife Rachel

Aldo scooping the pulp out of the machine

Around two years ago, before we'd each moved back from our respective lives across the other side of the country, the two elders of the cousins regrouped to bring back Tomato Day. It had been nearly two decades. Over that time, the original generation who passed on the food traditions that we celebrate today had all but disappeared. The overseers of the sauce, the bosses of the pasta, the masters of the spit roast, the holders of all biscuit and pastry secrets. Almost all of them have now passed away, or forgotten us. So, I do write this with a profound sense of loss.

Tomato Day, after all those years, was not just about the tomatoes: it was about acknowledging the end of something intangibly momentous, one of the deepest parts of my identity losing the people that tied it to the physical world. It turns out that reviving an old tradition adds a painful finality to what came before.

However, the immutable beauty of food traditions is that they're ultimately things of love. For all of the sadness and loss, there will always be greater amounts of happiness and hope. That first of the new Tomato Days coincided with our announcement of little Elio taking up tummy residence. Since then, our extended family has continued to grow, and we've all somehow found our way back home. We never stopped making pasta, but now we can make it together, with a whole new generation so full of life and laughter. And Tomato Day is looking good. We're gearing up for our biggest yet, with not one but two large concrete driveways to choose from. Here's to the future, and those tenacious little tomato plants that we'll find sprouting in the cracks for months to come.

TUTORIAL

Caramelle

A playful pasta, cut and pinched into
a lolly shape. Simple or decorative,
it's a great one to have some fun with.

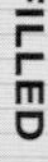

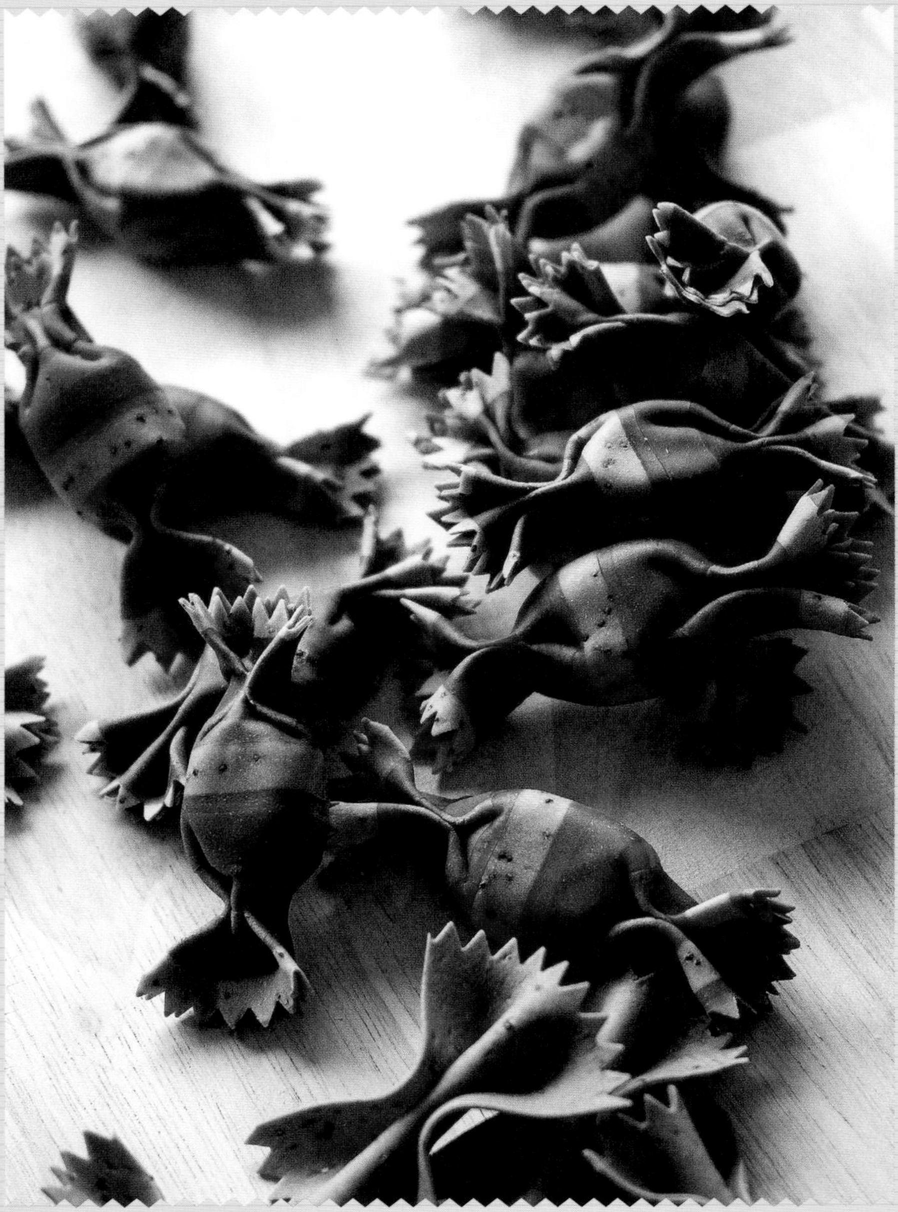

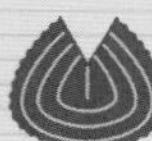

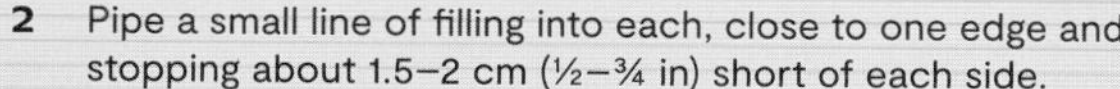

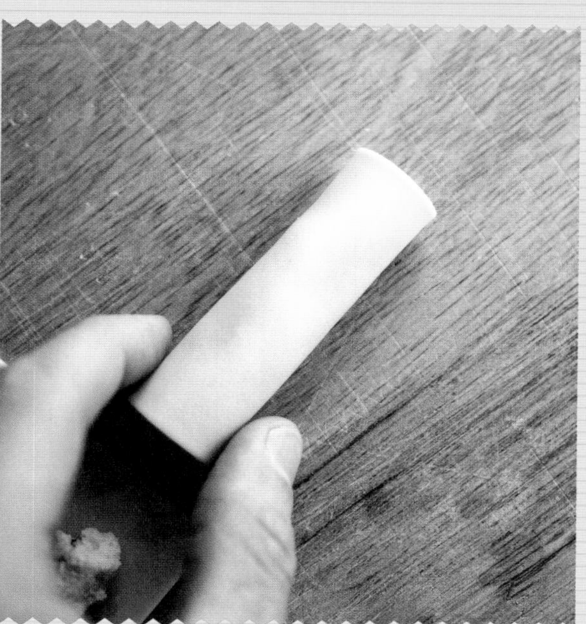

1 Cut 1 mm (1⁄16 in) thick sheets of egg dough (see page 18) into squares of approximately 6 cm (2½ in).

2 Pipe a small line of filling into each, close to one edge and stopping about 1.5–2 cm (½–¾ in) short of each side.

3 Roll the pasta up over the filling.

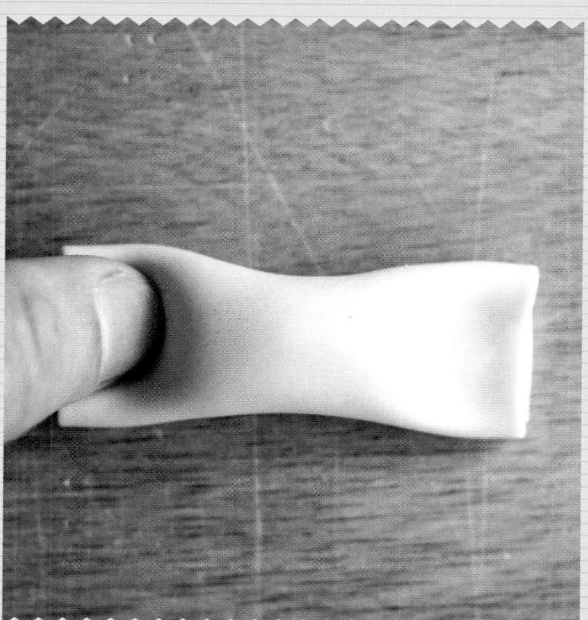

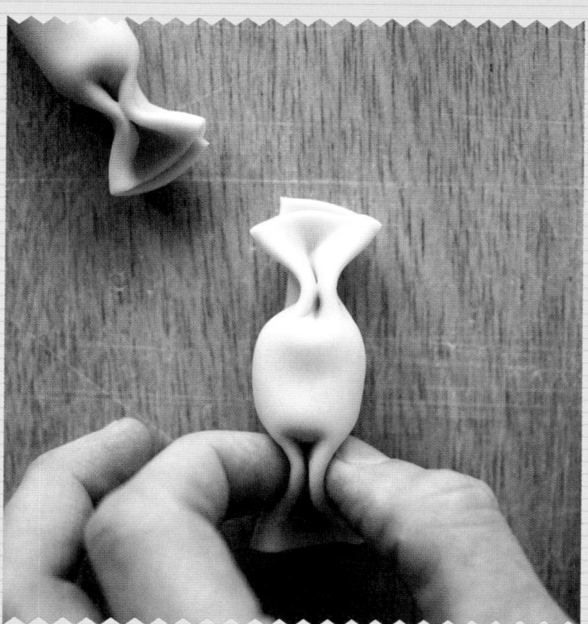

4 Then gently pinch each end around the filling to form into lolly-shaped caramelle.

5 If you have trouble sealing the dough, run a wet finger along the inside edge of the square where it overlaps.

Fig and anisette caramelle with gorgonzola and freeze-dried plum

SERVES 4 | TOTAL TIME 1 HR 5 MINS

One of the most enduring memories that I have of my nonna's house is actually my nonno's liqueur cabinet, filled with mysterious and intricate glassware, and the intoxicating smell of anisette. If I allowed Nonna five minutes of peace, she'd let me slide open the glass door and peer in. I think. Looking back now it seems unlikely that it was actually a sanctioned activity.

Forever competing for my fickle loyalty was my great aunty, who would keep a box of rectangular Italian lollies at the ready to coax me into fleeting compliance. And my mum, forever mediating the politics of leaving me with either relative for a day, has always had a soft spot for figs. From that disparate collection of influences was born our fig and anisette caramelle: an ode to the short-sighted rewards of bribing your children into good behaviour.

- 2 rosemary sprigs
- 8 fresh figs, quartered
- 2 tablespoons spiced agrumato (substitute with extra-virgin olive oil)
- 60 ml (2 fl oz/¼ cup) anisette liqueur
- 1 × quantity Egg yolk dough (page 18), made with 40 ml (1¼ fl oz) anisette liqueur (see page 21)
- 40 g (1½ oz) gorgonzola dolce, crumbled
- 2 teaspoons freeze-dried plum, crumbled

Prepare the filling by frying the rosemary and fig quarters in the agrumato over a medium–high heat, cut sides down, turning until lightly caramelised on all sides, about 2 minutes. Add the anisette to deglaze and cook for a further 30 seconds. Remove from the heat and allow to cool, discarding the rosemary and removing the figs, reserving the liquid. Blend the figs into a paste then transfer to a piping bag fitted with a medium round tip and refrigerate to firm up.

Roll the pasta out into sheets of around 1 mm (1⁄16 in) thickness (see Handmade pasta: Tutorial, page 33) and cut into 6 cm (2½ in) squares. Pipe a line of filling along one edge, and form into caramelle (see Caramelle: Tutorial, page 198). Store on lightly floured baking paper-lined trays until ready to cook.

Cook the pasta in lightly salted gently boiling water until done at the thickest join, 5–6 minutes, before tossing with the reserved agrumato. Use a little pasta water to help emulsification. Serve sprinkled with the gorgonzola and dried plum.

ON PASTA

You could really choose any filled shape as a substitute, but there's something special about caramelle. I just think that a playful shape works well with a playful filling. You'll notice that we've made these quite small, with less filling than usual. This is just a personal preference for this dish, but I do generally use smaller amounts of filling when working with punchier or bolder ingredients.

ON INGREDIENTS

It's really a very simple dish that depends on carefully handling the ingredients. Make sure that you achieve a gorgeous caramelisation on those figs, and the rest will fall into place.

Porcini and potato caramelle with white wine and guanciale

SERVES 4 | TOTAL TIME 1 HR 15 MINS

Potato inside pasta really is that good. For all of the creative things that you can cram inside a piece of pasta, sometimes simplest is best. This filling is made extra smooth and flavourful with the addition of ricotta, butter and dried porcini liquid. Served in a pasta alla Gricia–inspired sauce with little bits of crispy stuff to crunch alongside all of that squishiness.

- 440 g (15½ oz) potatoes, peeled and cubed
- 60 g (2 oz) smooth ricotta
- 1 small garlic clove, minced
- 15 g (½ oz) butter
- 1 small handful of chopped parsley
- 20 g (¾ oz) dried porcini, rehydrated in 100 ml (3½ fl oz) warm water for 20 minutes; discard the porcini, retain the liquid
- salt, freshly cracked black pepper and nutmeg, to taste
- 1 × quantity Whole egg and egg yolk dough (page 19)
- 100 g (3½ oz) guanciale, very thinly sliced
- 80 ml (2½ fl oz/⅓ cup) extra-virgin olive oil
- 120 g (4½ oz) fresh mushrooms, cut into thin strips
- 100 ml (3½ fl oz) white wine

To prepare the filling, begin by boiling the potatoes in lightly salted water for 15 minutes. Remove and allow to cool before ricing and mixing well with the ricotta, garlic, butter and parsley. Gradually pour in the porcini water, stirring, until the mixture can be whisked smooth without becoming runny (this should take most of the liquid). Season to taste, adding a touch of nutmeg, then transfer to a piping bag with a medium round tip.

Roll the pasta out into sheets of around 1 mm (1⁄16 in) thickness (see Handmade pasta: Tutorial, page 33) and cut into 8 cm (3¼ in) squares. Pipe a line of filling along one edge, and form into caramelle (see Caramelle: Tutorial, page 198).

Fry the guanciale using 2 tablespoons of the olive oil in a large frying pan over a medium–high heat until crispy, about 3–4 minutes. Remove and transfer to paper towel to drain.

In the same pan, fry the fresh mushrooms for 5–6 minutes (add another 2 tablespoons of olive oil if required), until they begin to shrink and darken. Add the wine, and allow to completely cook off.

Boil the caramelle in a large pot of salted water for 5–6 minutes until done, then scoop directly into the frying pan with 1–2 tablespoons of pasta water. Stir well to combine the oil and water into an emulsion, coating the pasta.

Serve with the guanciale crumbled on top and a crack of black pepper.

ON PASTA

This is another creamy filling for caramelle. More so than other filled shapes, you really notice lumps in caramelle, so I usually opt for a smooth filling. Any other filled shape works fine as a substitute, but I'm sucker for potato cappelletti (see page 222).

ON INGREDIENTS

The dried porcini really completes the flavour of this pasta, so while any mix of mushrooms works well for the sauce, make sure that you don't skip the porcini.

Balanzoni

Balanzoni are, for the most part, spinach tortellini with a ricotta-based filling. Nonna was famous for the same thing in ravioli form, and so we make our balanzoni on the larger and thicker side as a little nod to her. The shaping process is identical to what you would use for tortellini.

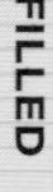

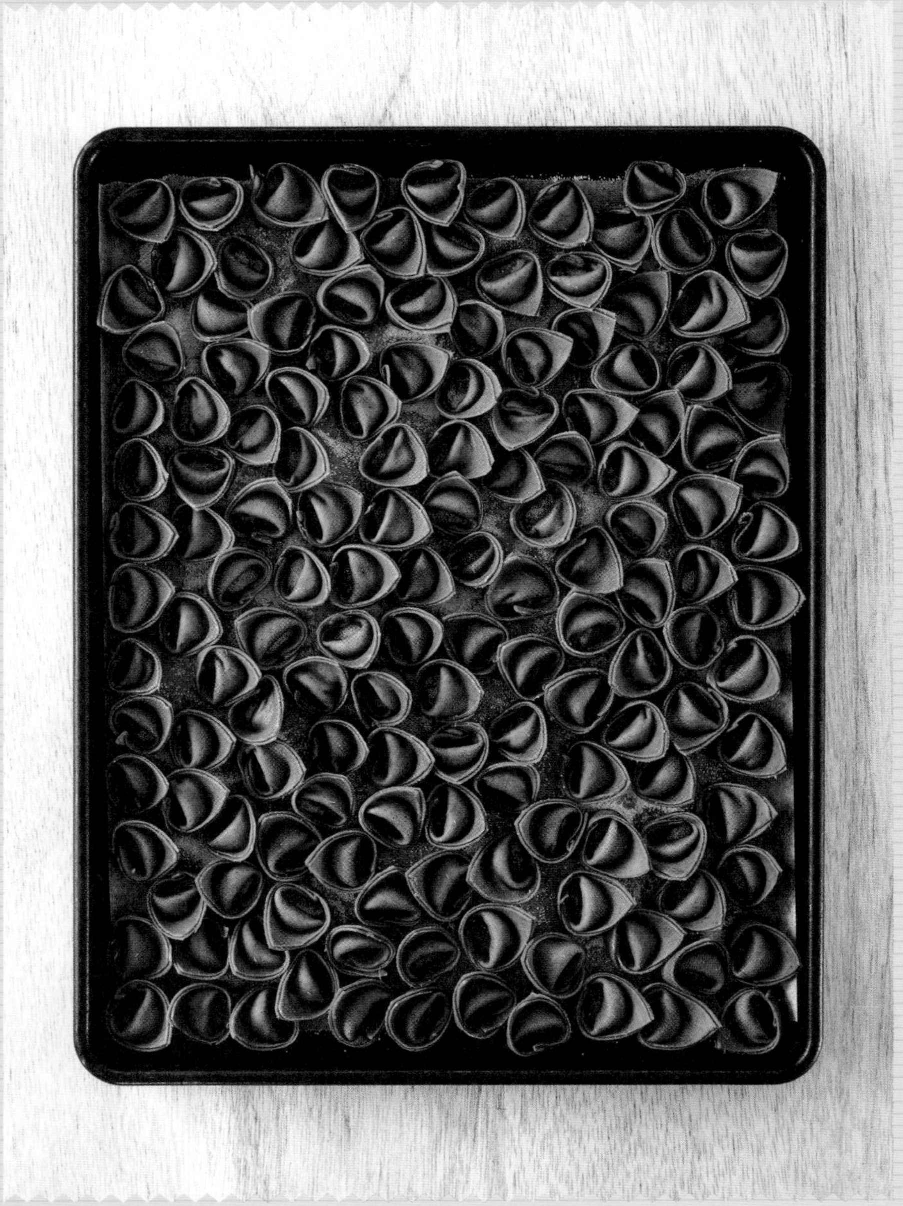

1 Cut sheets of 0.8–1 mm (1⁄16 in) thick Spinach dough (page 24) into squares of 4–5 cm (1½–2 in).

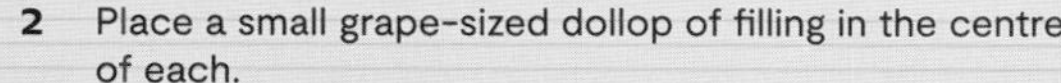

2 Place a small grape-sized dollop of filling in the centre of each.

3 Fold into triangles over the filling, then press gently along the edges to seal closed. Try to avoid trapping air.

4 Take one outer corner between your thumb and index finger as you roll the centre point of the triangle from an upright position to pointing down towards your wrist. You are aiming to create a little gentle fold along the bottom of the triangle.

5 Wrap the free outer corner around your thumb, overlapping it with the held corner, flat to the bottom edge. Press your fingers together.

Balanzoni with tomato and butter sauce

SERVES 4 | TOTAL TIME 1 HR 5 MINS

My dad used to bother and appal us all by adding butter to his sugo. Whenever he made the pasta sauce he'd have to weather abuse and wild Italian hand gestures from everyone. But we ate it. Then I grew up and gave it a little thought, and it turns out that he was on to something. I wouldn't go so far as to say that he was right, but in certain circumstances it does add a little velvety fattiness to the sauce, perfect with a handful of punchy dried herbs. Cook this one right down and it also makes for an excellent pizza sauce.

1 × quantity Spinach dough (page 24)

FILLING

- 375 g (13 oz/1½ cups) ricotta
- 100 g (3½ oz/2 cups) fresh baby spinach leaves, blanched, thoroughly drained and chopped (after blanching, this will reduce to around 50 g/1¾ oz/1 cup, so substitute accordingly if using frozen spinach)
- 1 egg
- 25 g (1 oz) Parmigiano Reggiano, grated, plus extra to serve
- salt, freshly cracked black pepper and nutmeg, to taste

SAUCE

- 2–3 garlic cloves, minced
- 2 tablespoons extra-virgin olive oil
- 700 ml (23½ fl oz) passata (puréed tomatoes)
- pinch each of dried basil, oregano, parsley, sage
- salt, freshly cracked black pepper and sugar, to taste
- 20 g (¾ oz) butter

To make the filling, mix together the ricotta, spinach, egg and cheese. Season to taste and transfer to a piping bag.

Roll the dough out into 0.8 mm (1⁄16 in) thick sheets (see Handmade pasta: Tutorial, page 33) and fill, forming into balanzoni (see Balanzoni: Tutorial, page 204).

Begin the sauce by gently sautéing the garlic very briefly in the olive oil. Use a large frying pan over a low heat and stir regularly to avoid browning. Add the passata and herbs, season to taste, then cook for 15–20 minutes.

Melt the butter into the sauce and cook for a further 2–3 minutes.

Boil the balanzoni in a large pot of salted water until done, 3–4 minutes, then scoop directly into the sauce. Add a little pasta water and stir well to combine, evenly coating the pasta.

Serve with freshly grated hard cheese and a crack of pepper.

ON PASTA

Ravioli (see page 172) is a slightly quicker and less fiddly alternative that works well with these same ingredients.

ON INGREDIENTS

For the flavour that still makes me pause and mouth wordless nothings over my pasta throughout the meal, make sure that you always use the freshest ricotta available. Though it's not my personal preference, many pasta makers love smooth ricotta for their fillings. If this is you, I'd recommend just whisking the filling ingredients together for a little longer to produce a creamier mixture.

Marbled balanzoni with fennel and pumpkin seed brown butter

SERVES 4 | TOTAL TIME 1 HR 5 MINS

The familiar flavour of fennel is found in many of our family dishes, both sweet and savoury. In fact, between the anethole-in-common fennel, anise, anise myrtle, star anise and liquorice, as well as the structurally similar tarragon and basil, we serve up very little without at least a touch of that subtle sweetness. Here in Australia, like so much that was cooked with back in Italy, fennel is an invasive species; but that can't dampen our inherited enthusiasm. Ironically, the more bulbous cultivated fennel that you buy at greengrocers is not as flavoursome as the original weed now plaguing bushland and roadsides, so we often supplement it with a handful of fennel seeds.

This recipe has the kind of efficiency that I appreciate after a long day, maybe with a glass of wine in hand. Heat the oven while you knead the dough, then roast the fennel while it rests. Mix up the filling, make the pasta, and finish the sauce while it boils. Pasta therapy.

- ½ × quantity Spinach dough (page 24)
- ½ × quantity Whole egg dough (page 18)

FILLING

- 400 g (14 oz) ricotta
- 50 g (1¾ oz) pecorino Romano, grated
- 1 egg
- pinch each of ground cloves, nutmeg and black pepper

SAUCE

- 300 g (10½ oz) fresh fennel, thinly sliced (this should reduce to around 120 g/4½ oz after roasting)
- 1 tablespoon extra-virgin olive oil
- 1 teaspoon fennel seeds
- salt and freshly cracked black pepper, to taste
- 100 g (3½ oz) butter
- 20 g (¾ oz) pepitas (pumpkin seeds)
- 2–3 mint leaves, crushed

Preheat the oven to 200°C (390°F). Toss the fennel with the olive oil, fennel seeds and a seasoning of salt and pepper, then roast for 25–30 minutes, turning and shuffling regularly. The fennel should soften and shrink, and begin to brown at the ends.

While the fennel cooks, prepare the balanzoni. Mix together the ricotta, pecorino, egg and spices until smooth; load into a piping bag.

Next, marble together the two pasta doughs (see Multi-coloured pasta: Tutorial, page 50) to a thickness of 0.8 mm (1⁄16 in); then cut and form into balanzoni (see Balanzoni: Tutorial, page 204).

In a large frying pan, melt the butter over a medium–high heat for 3–5 minutes until it begins to foam and turn brown. Add the fennel, pepitas and mint leaves, cooking for a further 1–2 minutes before removing from the heat.

Cook the balanzoni in a large pot of salted boiling water until done, about 3–4 minutes, and then use a slotted spoon to scoop directly into the frying pan with the brown butter. Add a little pasta water and stir to combine.

Serve with a crack of black pepper.

ON PASTA

We've gone for a very subtle gradation of colour with these by rerolling the dough over itself a few times before thinning it out. For bolder marbling, don't fold it.

ON INGREDIENTS

To halve the spinach dough in this recipe (which has an unhelpful number of eggs and yolks), simply use 2 eggs, adding a little more flour if it's too wet.

TUTORIAL

Tortelli

Tortelli generally refers to filled squares or circles folded in half with the outer corners brought together to meet, much like tortellini. There are all kinds of names for all kinds of shapes and endless disagreement that goes with it.

Here we are going to show you only two variations, both made from squares, although the next tutorial covers cappellacci, a sort of tortelli splinter-cell with its own variations (see Cappellacci: Tutorial, page 216).

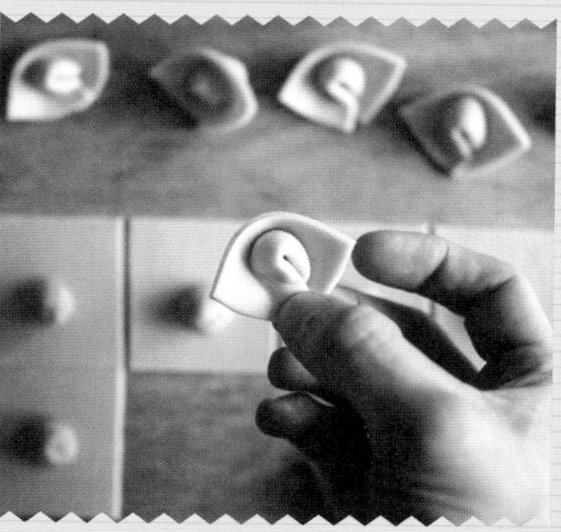

1 To make straight-edged tortelli, sometimes referred to as pansotti, cut fresh sheets of any egg pasta (see page 18), approximately 1 mm (1⁄16 in) thick, into squares. The size is really your preference, depending on the intensity of the filling and your intended eating experience. We generally make ours around 6 cm (2½ in) across. You can also make them stand up neatly like little boats by increasing how much the pinched corners overlap; personally, I prefer them in a lazy slouch.

2 Place a large dollop of filling in the middle of each, then fold in half, straight edge to straight edge, forming a rectangle with the filling in the centre. Press down on the overlapping dough to seal.

3 Poke gently in the side of the filling, and then bring the corners around the hollow that you just formed, overlapping slightly and pinching firmly to seal in place.

NOTE For offset tortelli, fold in half over the filling, offsetting it so that you are left with four corners on one side and a straight edge on the other.

Poke sideways on the flat edge, then draw the outer corners around the dimple formed, to overlap slightly. The angle of overlap should approximate the angle between the other corners. Press firmly to seal.

Eggplant and pecorino tortelli with 'nduja and tomato

SERVES 4 | TOTAL TIME 1 HR 15 MINS

Aldo and I once went into a fine foods providore sort of deli looking for 'nduja. He was about two and a half. As always, I let the little guy do the talking, and he eloquently asked 'excuse me, do you have any 'nduja?' The woman at the counter gave him a blank look over rows of imported salami. 'Do we have any what?' Without pause, he repeated ''nduja'. She looked at me pleadingly like he was speaking gibberish, so I mimed Italian hands for 'you heard the man, 'nduja!' And then we both bombarded her with ''nduja!' over and over until she gave up and stalked off.

If you know 'nduja, then you know 'nduja. The spicy, spreadable southern salami that makes everything better. And if you don't, then you have no business selling cold meats. Silver lining: it was a moment of bonding and solidarity, and we still occasionally yell ''nduja!' back and forth at each other in fond remembrance of frazzling that salami pretender.

1 × quantity Whole egg and egg yolk dough (page 19)

FILLING

800 g (1 lb 12 oz) whole eggplant (aubergine)

40 g (1½ oz) pecorino Romano, grated, plus extra to serve

20 g (¾ oz) breadcrumbs

juice and zest of ½ lemon

salt and freshly cracked black pepper, to taste

SAUCE

60 ml (2 fl oz/¼ cup) extra-virgin olive oil

1 small handful of basil leaves

6–8 sage leaves

4 garlic cloves, minced

700 ml (23½ fl oz) crushed tomatoes or passata (puréed tomatoes)

salt and freshly cracked black pepper, to taste

½ teaspoon sugar

60 g (2 oz) 'nduja (substitute with soft, chopped salami)

Begin with the filling. Bake the eggplant directly on an oven rack at 220°C (430°F) for 20 minutes. Scoop out the flesh and drain any excess water; discard the skin. Blend together with the pecorino, breadcrumbs, lemon juice and zest, and season; transfer to a piping bag with a medium round tip.

Next, heat the olive oil in a medium-hot frying pan and fry the basil and sage leaves for 5–10 seconds until crispy. Remove the leaves from the pan and drop the heat to low.

Sauté the garlic for 2–3 minutes, stirring, before adding the crushed tomato. Season with salt and sugar, and add the 'nduja, breaking it up with the spoon as you stir. Cook for 15–20 minutes, or until the sauce has thickened and the tomato has lost its raw flavour.

While the sauce cooks, roll the pasta dough out into 1 mm (1⁄16 in) sheets (see Handmade pasta: Tutorial, page 33) and cut into 6 cm (2½ in) squares. Squeeze a large, grape-sized dollop of filling into each and form into straight-edged tortelli (see Tortelli: Tutorial, page 211).

Boil the pasta until done, about 4–5 minutes, then use a slotted spoon to drop them directly into the sauce. Stir well, using a little pasta water to combine.

Serve with the crispy basil and sage leaves, plenty of grated hard cheese and freshly cracked black pepper.

ON PASTA

The square-edged folds on these tortelli are particularly good at holding sauce, but play around with other tortelli shapes for something different. Cappellacci (see page 216), really a type of tortelli themselves, are a great substitute.

ON INGREDIENTS

Although it channels Ma's eggplant (aubergine) parmigiana, we roast our eggplant instead of frying it, just to avoid an overly oily filling. If you'd prefer to fry them up though, just blot a bit of that oil out before blending.

Roasted garlic tortelli with lamb ragù

SERVES 4 | TOTAL TIME 4 HRS 15 MINS

When Rachel and I were in the town of Ella in beautiful Sri Lanka many years ago, we came across garlic curry. It was one of a myriad curries brought to us from behind a red velvet curtain that transformed the chef's living room into his restaurant. For someone who buys upwards of half a dozen garlic bulbs at a time, a dish that essentially swaps its major protein component for garlic was a surprisingly revelatory discovery.

Since then, I have only become more unashamed in my employment of the humble garlic clove. Roasted until soft, it takes on a gorgeous deep flavour, and loses much of its pungency. Stir it into ricotta with a finely grated hard cheese, and you have an unfussy pasta filling of mellow joy. Perfect for just about any sauce, especially a flavourful lamb ragù.

1 × quantity Whole egg and egg yolk dough (page 19)

FILLING

- 100 g (3½ oz) garlic, as whole bulbs
- 300 g (10½ oz) ricotta
- 50 g (1¾ oz) Parmigiano Reggiano, finely grated, plus extra to serve
- salt and freshly cracked black pepper, to taste

RAGÙ

- 2 tablespoons extra-virgin olive oil
- 400 g (14 oz) boneless lamb leg, diced and patted dry
- 4 garlic cloves, roughly chopped
- 1 onion, diced
- 1 carrot, diced
- 1 celery stalk, roughly chopped
- 1 tablespoon tomato paste (concentrated purée)
- 100 ml (3½ fl oz) red wine
- 800 g (1 lb 12 oz) crushed tomatoes
- 400 ml (13½ fl oz) beef stock
- 2 bay leaves
- 2 rosemary sprigs
- 1 thyme sprig
- salt and freshly cracked black pepper, to taste

Preheat the oven to 200°C (390°F). Leave the garlic bulbs whole, but cut off the very tops and cover loosely with aluminium foil. Roast in the oven until soft, about 30–35 minutes. Remove and allow to cool.

Lower the oven to 180°C (360°F). Use the oil to brown the lamb in a heavy flameproof casserole over a medium–high heat. Work in batches if necessary to avoid crowding; it should only take 4–5 minutes. Remove to a plate.

Drop the heat to low–medium and, in the same casserole, gently sauté the garlic, onion, carrot and celery for 10–15 minutes. Stir regularly to avoid it catching or browning. Add the tomato paste and cook for another 2–3 minutes before deglazing with the wine.

Once the wine has mostly evaporated, add the lamb back in, along with the tomatoes, stock and herbs; season to taste. Cover the casserole and transfer to the oven for 2–3 hours, or until the meat can be gently pulled apart with a fork. Keep an eye on the moisture and add water as necessary.

To make the pasta filling, use a little gentle pressure to squeeze the roasted garlic out of the bulbs and stir into the ricotta with the cheese. Season to taste and load into a piping bag.

Roll the pasta dough out into 1 mm (1⁄16 in) thick sheets (see Handmade pasta: Tutorial, page 33), cut into 6 cm (2½ in) squares and use the filling to form into offset tortelli (see Tortelli: Tutorial, page 211).

Boil the tortelli in a large pot of salted water for 4–5 minutes, or until done, then use a slotted spoon to scoop directly into the ragù; reserve a cup of pasta water. Add enough of the pasta water into the ragù, as you stir it together with the tortelli, to produce a smooth sauce that clings to the pasta.

Serve with grated hard cheese and cracked black pepper.

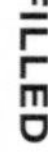

ON PASTA

This is such a smooth, creamy filling that you can really fill any pasta with it. For something a bit different, try ravioli (see page 172). Alternatively, with a hearty sauce like this, opt for an unfilled pasta as a substitute. Pappardelle (see page 34) and malloreddus (see page 142) are excellent choices, depending on which way you want to take it.

ON INGREDIENTS

No, it's not too much garlic. For even asking that question, add another head of it.

Cappellacci

A type of tortelli, this easy and versatile shape has earned its own category, complete with its own variations. This chapter includes two methods of making them.

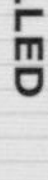

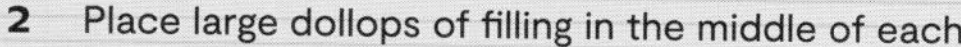

1 Begin with 1 mm (1⁄16 in) thick sheets of egg dough (see page 18) cut into squares of between 6–8 cm (2½–3¼ in).

2 Place large dollops of filling in the middle of each.

3 Unlike our straight-edged and offset tortelli, fold these in half over the filling to form triangles. Poke the inner edge of the filling to form a dimple,

4 Then bring the outer corners of the triangle around it to overlap slightly. Pinch the overlap to seal in place.

NOTE Another fun way to make these is to cut into semicircles after filling and folding, bringing the corners together to form plumper, rounded cappellacci (see page 220).

Red wine cappellacci with sage brown butter

SERVES 4 | TOTAL TIME 55 MINS

Though this book includes a few butter finishes, we've continued to dance around the classic sage brown butter; well here it is. With a pasta dough rich from wine and a filling of meat and herbs, there really are few sauce options that won't overcomplicate the pasta, let alone lift it up. As with all brown butter recipes, keep an eye on that foam. Once it starts to disappear, the browning will speed up considerably. You can scoop out the solids for a more refined sauce, but personally I find it takes most of the flavour with it and so prefer to leave all those little bits and pieces in.

- 300 g (10½ oz) minced (ground) beef
- 1 tablespoon extra-virgin olive oil
- 1 tarragon sprig
- 1 rosemary sprig
- 100 g (3½ oz) ricotta
- 50 g (1¾ oz) pecorino Romano, grated, plus extra to serve
- salt and freshly cracked black pepper, to taste
- 1 × quantity Red wine dough (page 24)
- 100 g (3½ oz) butter
- 1 handful of sage leaves

To make the filling, brown the beef in the olive oil with the tarragon and rosemary over a medium–high heat for 10–15 minutes, or until beginning to crisp. Remove and allow to cool before blending to a smooth, spoonable consistency with the ricotta and pecorino. Season to taste and transfer to a piping bag.

Roll the red wine dough into 1 mm (1⁄16 in) thick sheets (see Handmade pasta: Tutorial, page 33) and use the filling to form cappellacci (see Cappellacci: Tutorial, page 216).

Next, in a large frying pan, melt the butter over a medium–high heat for 1–2 minutes. Add the sage leaves and cook for a further 3–4 minutes, or until the butter browns.

Cook the pasta in a large pot of salted water for 3–4 minutes until done, then spoon directly into the brown butter. Stir well, and use a little pasta water to create an emulsion with the sauce.

Serve simply with a crack of pepper and maybe even that familiar mountain of grated hard cheese.

ON PASTA

Make sure that you refer to the recipe for directions on reducing the red wine. You could mix it in unreduced, but it won't retain that rich velvety colour and flavour after boiling. Served in a simple butter sauce, any pasta would work as a substitute, with the closest being tortelli (see page 211).

ON INGREDIENTS

Take the opportunity to completely overhaul the flavour profile of this filling by swapping in your favourite herbs. We sometimes go for the old parsley, sage, rosemary, and thyme combination.

Spiralled asparagus and mascarpone cappellacci with red cabbage broth

SERVES 4 | TOTAL TIME 1 HR 10 MINS

One of little Al's favourite things in life is our weekend trip to the markets, and it's become one of mine too. We start with a snack and a coffee, a decaf macchiato for him and a double espresso for me, then head to the butcher, deli, seafood shop, wholefoods shop and, finally, the greengrocer. He's famous for running crazed laps through the store and weaving wildly between shoppers as I track him over the displays by watching for erratic behaviour amongst the taller patrons. But he's also known for his discerning and creative eye when it comes to selecting our fresh produce.

It's a simple thing, letting him choose an ingredient, take it home, cook it and eat it, but the satisfaction on his face for this little bit of world-mastery is worth all of the hasty apologies to his crash victims and the beating that I occasionally receive at the end of a stick of lemongrass. While I can't guarantee consistency in every two-year-old's shopping list, Aldo definitely earns the spirals in these cappellacci. This ingredient list is chosen entirely by him.

½ × quantity Whole egg dough (page 18)

½ × quantity Spinach dough (page 24)

FILLING

160 g (5½ oz) asparagus

280 g (10 oz) mascarpone

70 g (2½ oz) breadcrumbs

salt, to taste

BROTH

600 g (1 lb 5 oz) red cabbage, roughly chopped

1 onion, roughly chopped

4 garlic cloves, smashed

1 teaspoon black peppercorns

1 tablespoon extra-virgin olive oil

600 ml (20½ fl oz) vegetable stock

1 small handful of parsley

4 bay leaves

1 teaspoon salt

TO PLATE

50 g (1¾ oz/⅓ cup) crumbled feta

1 zucchini (courgette), ribboned

1 handful of roasted pistachios

1 small handful of micro-herbs

To make the broth, sauté the red cabbage, onion, garlic and peppercorns in the olive oil in a pot set over a medium heat for 10 minutes, stirring regularly. Once the onion begins to soften and turn translucent, add the stock, parsley, bay leaves and salt, then simmer over a low–medium heat for a further 15–20 minutes. Remove from the heat and strain out the broth. To make the most of your ingredients, consider retaining the cabbage to serve as a side. We often toss it with some blanched greens, olive oil, crumbled feta and lemon juice.

Prepare the filling by blanching the asparagus in boiling water for 2–3 minutes. Set aside the tips for plating, then blend the stalks with the mascarpone, breadcrumbs and salt. Note that you can retain the asparagus cooking water to later cook the pasta in. Transfer the blended filling to a piping bag fitted with a medium round tip.

Roll both pasta doughs out into sheets of around 1 mm (1⁄16 in) thickness (see Handmade pasta: Tutorial, page 33), and then proceed to create spiralled discs of dough (see Multi-coloured pasta: Tutorial, page 53); final thickness of 1 mm (1⁄16 in), around 8 cm in diameter.

Squeeze a grape-sized amount of filling into the centre of each piece and fold in half using your fingers to press down around the filling and seal the pasta. Use a fluted circle cutter to cut a semicircle around the filling, with the dough fold on the straight side, then bring the corners around the filling to meet and form cappellacci (see Cappellacci: Tutorial, page 216).

Drop the cappellacci into lightly salted boiling water and cook for 4–5 minutes, until done. Drain and serve in the broth with the asparagus tips, crumbled feta, zucchini ribbons, pistachios and micro-herbs.

ON PASTA

Caramelle (see page 198) are a really fun substitute that work well with both the filling and the colourful spirals.

ON INGREDIENTS

To halve the spinach dough in this recipe, use 2 eggs, adding a little more flour if it's too wet.

TUTORIAL

Cappelletti

Similar to cappellacci, these doughy little hats seem to work perfectly however you fill them, and with whatever they're served in.

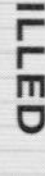

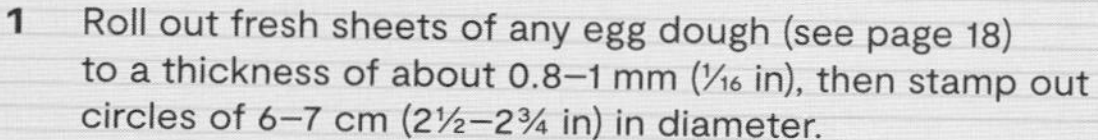

1 Roll out fresh sheets of any egg dough (see page 18) to a thickness of about 0.8–1 mm (1/16 in), then stamp out circles of 6–7 cm (2½–2¾ in) in diameter.

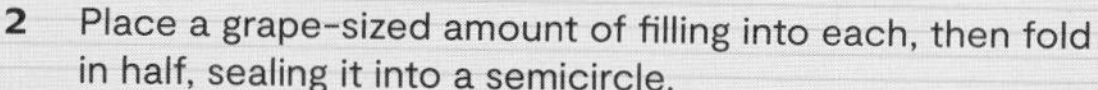

2 Place a grape-sized amount of filling into each, then fold in half, sealing it into a semicircle.

3 Gently poke the centre sideways towards the curved edge, then bring the corners around the filling to overlap slightly. Make sure that the edges leading to the overlapping corners are flat to each other to avoid accidental cappellacci (see page 216).

4 Pinch lightly to complete the shape.

Braised short-rib cappelletti in fennel broth

SERVES 8 | TOTAL TIME 6 HRS 30 MINS

One of our favourite pasta sauces is slow-cooked short-rib ragù. With a little wild boar salami, plenty of tomatoes and a nice big cup of wine it's a rich and deeply flavoursome dish. Possibly the only way to improve on it is to reduce it right down and stick it inside some pasta, which is precisely what we've done with these cappelletti.

While lighter, ricotta-filled pasta can easily pair with a heavier sauce, if you're inverting a rich ragù-pasta relationship like this, then those flavour-packed parcels will benefit from a thin, subtly flavoured sauce or broth. This one's a big hit with our youngest pastaio.

- 80 ml (2½ fl oz/⅓ cup) extra-virgin olive oil
- 1 kg (2 lb 3 oz) short ribs, on the bone and cut into short lengths
- 1 teaspoon salt
- 1 teaspoon freshly cracked black pepper
- 1 onion, diced
- 1 carrot, diced
- 2 celery stalks, diced
- 4 garlic cloves, roughly chopped
- 80 g (2¾ oz) wild boar and fennel salami, diced (substitute with other salami)
- 200 ml (7 fl oz) red wine
- 700 ml (23½ fl oz) passata (puréed tomatoes)
- 1 large rosemary sprig
- 2 bay leaves
- 300 ml (10 fl oz) beef bone broth or stock (see page 192)
- 2 teaspoons paprika
- salt, freshly cracked black pepper and sugar, to taste
- 2 × quantities Whole egg dough (page 18)
- grated hard cheese, to serve

FENNEL BROTH

- 300 g (10½ oz) fennel, roughly chopped (retain the fronds)
- 1 teaspoon fennel seeds
- 3 tablespoons extra-virgin olive oil
- 1 onion, roughly chopped
- 1 carrot, roughly chopped
- 1 celery stalk, roughly chopped
- 2 garlic cloves, roughly chopped
- 1 teaspoon black peppercorns
- salt, to taste

Preheat the oven to 180°C (360°F). To make the broth, toss together the fennel, fennel seeds and 1 tablespoon of olive oil on a baking tray and roast in the oven for 25–30 minutes until the fennel begins to brown.

While that cooks, gently fry the onion, carrot, celery and garlic in the remaining olive oil in a large pot. Stir regularly over a medium heat for 15–20 minutes until the vegetables have begun to soften and brown. Add the roasted fennel and fennel seeds, the retained fennel fronds, 1.5 litres (51 fl oz/6 cups) water and the peppercorns, adding salt to taste. Bring to the boil before dropping to a medium heat and partially covering. Cook for 45–50 minutes, then strain well.

Lower the oven to 160°C (320°F). Pour 1 tablespoon of olive oil into a large enamelled cast-iron pot set over a medium–high heat. Pat the short ribs dry with paper towel, then rub with 1 teaspoon of salt and the pepper before dropping into the pot. You may need to cook them in small batches to maintain the heat. Remove once browned, and lower the heat.

Add the remaining oil to the pot, along with the onion, carrot, celery, garlic and salami. Cook over a low heat for 15–20 minutes, stirring regularly.

Once the onion begins to turn translucent and the other ingredients start to brown, add the ribs back in and pour in the wine to deglaze the pot. Allow to cook down until mostly evaporated, then add the passata, herbs and stock, seasoning with the paprika, a pinch of sugar, and salt and pepper to taste. Cover the pot and transfer to the oven. Cook for 4–5 hours, adding small amounts of water if it becomes too dry.

Remove from the oven and skim off any visible fat. Lift out the ribs, discarding the bones, and shred. Add enough liquid back into the meat to leave it soft and juicy, but able to hold together enough for use as a pasta filling. Be sure to retain the leftover sauce, as it makes for a fantastic meal in its own right.

Roll the pasta dough to a thickness of around 1 mm (1⁄16 in) (see Handmade pasta: Tutorial, page 33), then use the short-rib filling to form cappelletti (see Cappelletti: Tutorial, page 222).

Return the broth to the boil, then drop the cappelletti in for 4–5 minutes, or until done. Serve in the fennel broth with a fresh crack of pepper and grated hard cheese on top.

ON PASTA

I'll be honest, the lazy and completely honourable alternative is to simply lift out the bones, mash it all together and serve it as an incredible ragù with just about any pasta you feel like.

ON INGREDIENTS

The liquid left over from cooking the ribs makes for an excellent sauce in its own right. In fact, meat like this is traditionally served as a separate course alongside the pasta, which is stirred through the sauce. Refrigerate it for 2–3 days, or freeze immediately, and it will make for an incredibly gourmet short-notice sugo.

Peperonata cappelletti with sausage ragù

SERVES 4 | TOTAL TIME 2 HRS 25 MINS

One of my ma's greatest dishes, that still stops me in my tracks and has me annoyingly picking at it all the way from the oven to the table, is her humble peperonata. Another Italian dish that's very open to interpretation, ours is simply capsicums (bell peppers) and potatoes roasted with a good hit of olive oil and tossed in breadcrumbs. You can't go wrong. We've taken that magic combination as inspiration for these cappelletti.

Fussier pasta is well suited to a simpler sauce, and sausage ragù is one of our guilty fallbacks when we're pressed for time. My great aunty's sausage sauce was basically the best thing north of the Swan River, and is the origin of our contemporary ragù. Unlike ours, with the meat squeezed out and fried, she would deftly twist her sausages into tiny lengths and boil them whole in the sauce. I've never been able to match that incredible flavour, but I tell myself that it's because butchers just aren't what they used to be, and make a pointedly different but equally delicious sausage ragù instead.

1 × quantity Whole egg dough (page 18)

FILLING

- 200 g (7 oz) potato, chopped into thick batons
- 200 g (7 oz) red capsicum (bell pepper), sliced
- 40 g (1½ oz) breadcrumbs
- 2 garlic cloves, minced
- 2 tablespoons extra-virgin olive oil
- 40 g (1½ oz) ricotta
- salt and freshly cracked black pepper, to taste

SAUCE

- 1 garlic bulb, peeled and smashed
- 1 onion, diced
- 2 tablespoons extra-virgin olive oil
- 1 teaspoon dried chilli flakes (optional)
- 1 rosemary sprig
- 1 teaspoon fennel seeds
- 5–6 large sage leaves
- 400 g (14 oz) Italian sausages
- 400 g (14 oz) tinned diced tomatoes
- 400 g (14 oz) tinned cherry tomatoes
- 1 teaspoon sugar
- salt and freshly cracked black pepper, to taste

Begin with the pasta filling. Preheat the oven to 180°C (360°F). Toss together on a baking tray the potato, capsicum, breadcrumbs, garlic and olive oil and roast in the oven for 1 hour, shuffling once or twice. Remove and allow to cool, leaving the oven on.

Once cool, blend coarsely, then stir gently into the ricotta, seasoning to taste. Roll the pasta dough to a thickness of around 1 mm (1⁄16 in) and cut into 6 cm (2½ in) circles (see Handmade pasta: Tutorial, page 33), then use the peperonata filling to form cappelletti (see Cappelletti: Tutorial, page 222).

Next, for the sauce, add the smashed garlic, onion and oil to a large, enamelled cast-iron pot, and gently fry over a medium heat for 10 minutes. Stir regularly and don't allow it to brown.

Add the chilli flakes (if using), rosemary, fennel and sage, and cook for a further 2–3 minutes. Squeeze the sausage meat out of the casings and crumble or break into small pieces. Raise the heat to medium–high, and add the meat to the pot. Cook, stirring occasionally, for 5–10 minutes, until the meat has browned with a few crispy bits here and there.

Stir in the diced and cherry tomatoes, with the sugar. Season to taste with salt and pepper, and drop the heat to low. Cook, partially covered and stirring occasionally, for 20 minutes, allowing the sauce to reduce.

Transfer the pot to the oven, covered, for a further 20 minutes. If the sauce becomes too thick or dry, add a little water.

Cook the cappelletti in salted boiling water for 3–4 minutes until done, and then use a slotted spoon to transfer directly to the sauce. Stir well, and serve with grated hard cheese and a crack of black pepper.

ON PASTA

I wouldn't normally say to blend potato, unless you're after a poor glue substitute, but by blitzing it together with the other roasted ingredients then stirring the ricotta in last, you'll end up with a smooth but not overly starchy mixture.

ON INGREDIENTS

Do what the old uncles would do and drive 50 minutes across town to the butcher that does the best Italian sausages. They make or break this ragù.

TUTORIAL

Scarpinocc

One of the most intriguing and uniquely formed shapes in the pasta world, these little shoes are made with a fold, a roll, a pinch and a poke.

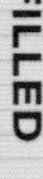

1 Lay out fresh sheets of any egg dough (see page 18) 0.8–1 mm (1⁄16 in) in thickness and stamp out circles of around 8 cm (3¼ in) in diameter.

2 Place a walnut-sized amount of filling in the centre of each.

3 Fold the dough in half over the filling, then press gently around it to seal.

4 Roll the filled centre of the pasta over so that the dough seam is now located underneath the pasta, off-centre.

5 Pinch the ends vertically to seal and, as you do so, also push downwards to set the pasta in its upright position.

6 Gently poke the top of each piece to form small dimples and give them their characteristic clog-like appearance.

Caramelised onion and taleggio scarpinocc with blackberry wild thyme reduction

SERVES 4 | TOTAL TIME 3 HRS

The question that I'm inevitably asked whenever we try something a bit different is 'what would Nonna think?' It's a hard question to answer, because, really, I think it misses the point of why we make pasta. My food philosophy, inherited from my family, is informed and sometimes expressed in classic dishes, but it isn't overly concerned with them. Instead, it's about how food is made and enjoyed.

I tell my boys that playfulness in cooking is how we discover and express ourselves. We learn how ingredients and processes work, we practise what we know to be good, and with all of that we create something of our own. Experimentation can bring mindfulness and reflection to a food tradition, and it helps us to live in the present as part of a long and sprawling culinary history, even if that history's only just beginning. Plus, classics aren't going anywhere; they'll keep looking after themselves.

So, I like to think that Nonna would approve. She might not love everything that we make, but I'm sure she'd love the fact that we're making it. Food should be prepared with honesty, creativity and love. Cook with that in mind and no nonna will begrudge you a little blackberry on your scarpinocc.

1 × quantity Egg yolk dough (page 18)

FILLING

- 400 g (14 oz) onion, sliced
- 2 tablespoons extra-virgin olive oil
- ½ teaspoon salt
- 120 g (4½ oz) taleggio
- 120 g (4½ oz) mascarpone

REDUCTION AND PARMESAN CRISPS

- 1 garlic clove, chopped
- 1 tablespoon extra-virgin olive oil
- 200 g (7 oz) fresh or frozen blackberries
- 80 ml (2½ fl oz/⅓ cup) balsamic vinegar
- 1½ teaspoons dried wild thyme
- ½ teaspoon black peppercorns
- salt and pepper, to taste
- 80 g (2¾ oz) Parmigiano Reggiano, grated

Gently caramelise the onions in the olive oil with the salt in a large frying pan over a low heat for 1 hour, stirring regularly. Drain off and retain the excess oil, and allow the onion to cool before blending it with the taleggio and mascarpone to form the filling. Transfer to a piping bag fitted with a medium round tip.

Prepare the pasta dough to a thickness of around 1 mm (1/16 in) (see Handmade pasta: Tutorial, page 33) and then cut into 8 cm (3¼ in) rounds. Use the filling to form scarpinocc (see Scarpinocc: Tutorial, page 228).

To make the reduction (which can be done while the onion caramelises), gently sauté the garlic in the olive oil for 2–3 minutes over a low heat, then add the blackberries. Raise the heat to medium and cook for a further 4–5 minutes, mashing up the berries with a wooden spoon.

Pour in the balsamic vinegar and allow to reduce by around half before adding 200 ml (7 fl oz) water, 1 teaspoon wild thyme and the peppercorns. Season to taste, then cook for 45–50 minutes, uncovered. The reduction will be ready when it sticks to the back of a spoon, holding its own when a finger is drawn through it.

For the parmesan crisps, preheat the oven to 200°C (390°F) and simply arrange the cheese on a baking tray lined with baking paper, sprinkle with the remaining wild thyme and bake in the oven for 6 minutes.

Cook the pasta in a large pot of boiling salted water for 4–5 minutes until done. Toss in the oil retained from cooking the onions and serve with the blackberry wild thyme reduction and parmesan crisps.

ON PASTA

We also love this filling in caramelle (see page 198), although it does make for a slightly fiddlier substitute.

ON INGREDIENTS

There's a mulberry tree that grows at my grandparents' old house, probably at least as old as my parents, and we still collect buckets of mulberries from it every year. When the season's right, they make an incredible substitution for frozen blackberries.

Lemon and poppy seed scarpinocc with citrus-infused olive oil

SERVES 4 | TOTAL TIME 45 MINS

To my dearest boys,

Aldo, you were barely two when we first made this dish for your ma, on Valentine's Day. From the start, you were an expert at giving scarpinocc their little poke in the middle, and they quickly became your favourite pasta shape. By the time you turned three, you could make them from scratch. You're a kind and thoughtful soul, but bursting with energy and a little boisterous mischief. Somehow scarpinocc seems like the right shape for you.

Elio, I don't know yet what your favourite shape will be, but no doubt something that reflects your quiet determination, eternal cheeriness and preference for a more silent kind of mischief than Aldo. For now, you're following in your brother's footsteps and showing quite the aptitude for scrunching and throwing a wide variety of shapes.

You two probably won't recall these early floury moments that we're sharing when you're old and evidently sentimental like me, but this only fills me with joy. You'll likely never remember the first time that you set foot in the kitchen, or made pasta, because this little tradition of ours will have been with you for longer than your memory serves. As it has been with me. Keep cooking from the heart, and always eat well.

I love you,

Dad.

- 120 ml (4 fl oz) extra-virgin olive oil
- peel of 1 lemon
- peel of 1 orange
- 400 g (14 oz) ricotta
- zest of 1 lemon
- salt and freshly cracked black pepper, to taste
- 1 × quantity Egg yolk dough (page 18), made with 2 tablespoons lemon juice and 1 tablespoon poppy seeds (see page 21)
- 1 small handful of freeze-dried sour cherries
- 2 teaspoons pink peppercorns

Warm the olive oil, lemon and orange peel in a small pot over a very low heat for 10–15 minutes. Remove and allow to cool. Lift out and finely slice the peel; retain for plating.

Next, prepare the filling by mixing together the ricotta, lemon zest and a little salt and pepper. Transfer to a piping bag with a medium round tip.

Roll the dough out into sheets of 0.8–1 mm (1⁄16 in) thickness (see Handmade pasta: Tutorial, page 33), then cut into circles of around 8 cm (3¼ in) in diameter. Pipe a walnut-sized amount of filling into the centre of each circle and form into scarpinocc (see Scarpinocc: Tutorial, page 228).

Cook the pasta in lightly salted boiling water for 4–5 minutes until done. Drain lightly, and toss in the citrus oil, mixing well to emulsify the water and oil. If you're concerned about breaking the pasta, simply whisk together a little pasta water with the oil before stirring in the scarpinocc. Serve with freeze-dried sour cherries, the retained peel, pink peppercorns and a crack of black pepper.

ON PASTA

Doughs with lumpy things in them like this can be harder to cut and form, but scarpinocc is a versatile shape and you'll have no issue getting them adequately cut and sealed. If substituting, simpler shapes like mezzalune or triangoli work well, and simpler folded shapes like cappellacci (see page 216) also demand less of the dough.

ON INGREDIENTS

These are very gentle, mild flavours, although nicely complemented by the sour cherries and pink peppercorns. If you can't find sour cherries, try a splash of balsamic vinegar instead.

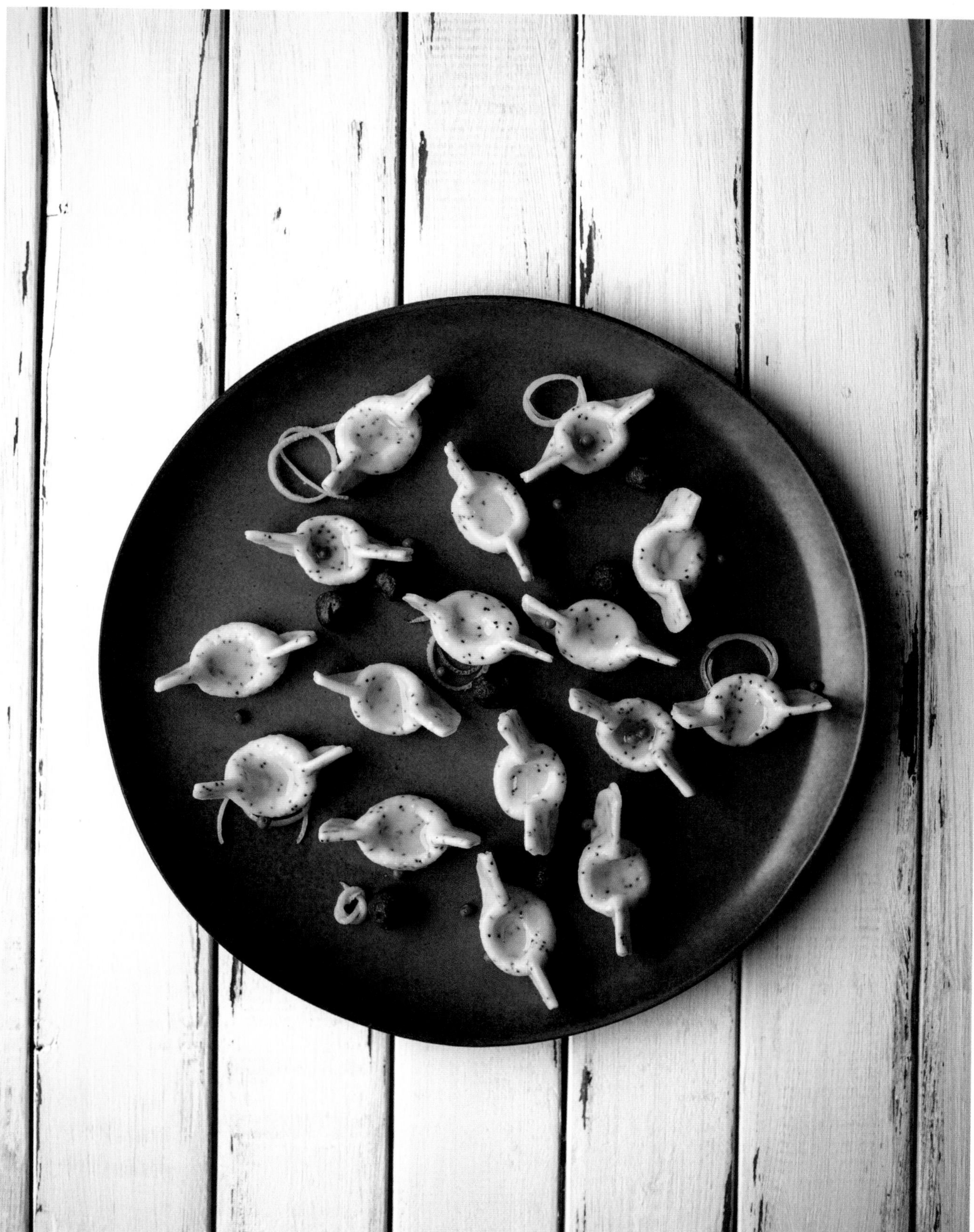

Epilogue

On the hunt for the last ingredient to cook the final dish for this book, I found myself incidentally parking behind a sprawling cemetery. I'd only been back in Perth a few months and was still rediscovering my old town, but as I pulled to a stop by the gate I suddenly realised where I was. I retraced the steps that I used to walk with Nonna, usually at the end of a long and well-travelled train trip, and found Nonno's grave.

I sat on the grass for some time, struggling through the uniquely sombre yet grounding emotion that loss offers us. It wasn't so much grief for Nonno himself as it was for a whole time and place in my life. The surrounding headstones were familiar with the names of relatives, family friends and strangers who I remember deciding as a child must share some kind of silent allegiance with Nonno. His headstone was unchanged, though I don't know why I expected any different.

I left briefly, to drive around in mounting rain and frustration, until I finally found a candle to replace the melted-out tea light in his lantern. It was apparently foolish to presume there'd be a market for chandlers in the vicinity of cemeteries. The downpour abated as I returned and, standing back after relighting his little flame, golden sunlight broke through the clouds to hit the speckled stone. I was immediately back by Nonna's side, as if those times had only ever been a small step away. Maybe they had.

I stood there a little longer, kissed his photo like Nonna had taught me. And then I went home to my family and made pasta.

Nonno, shortly after arriving in Perth, circa 1955

Me, aged 3, carrying flowers to Nonno's grave

Acknowledgements

The boys may have made it into the dedication, but to my wife, Rachel, goes my deepest gratitude and respect. You've thrown boundless support and enthusiasm behind *Pasta et Al* since its earliest days. This book, written over the most undeniably difficult period of our lives together, would never have grown beyond a fleeting daydream without you behind it. I promise that you will always have fresh pasta on Sunday.

Ma, Antonietta: Nonna may have taught me fettuccine and ravioli, but you taught me food. The old girl got you on the technicality, otherwise this would have been a book about your tradition, not hers. Thank you.

To the wonderful online community that has grown with us, buoyed us on, cooked our recipes, been inspired by our stories: grazie mille. You showed us that an odd little blend of introspective anecdotes and pasta can connect a sprawling international audience. I hope that we continue to inspire you, and that whatever food traditions you practise, they bring only love and joy into your lives.

To the team that made it happen, I'm honoured by your belief in us. You've helped to turn this humble weekly thing that we do into a beautiful book. It now holds a place in the very food history that I write about. So, to my publisher Michael Harry, my editor Antonietta Melideo, copyeditor Andrea O'Connor, and all of the Hardie Grant editorial, design and marketing staff involved, my sincere thanks. And, of course, Evi-O.Studio, I can't imagine this book designed by anyone else.

Finally, to everyone else who we've encountered on this long and unexpected adventure. Those who tested recipes, those who shared meals, and those who offered even the most fleeting words of encouragement. May your pasta always be made with love and cooked to perfection.

Index

Entries in *italics* indicate tutorials

P

R

S

T

V

W

Z

Published in 2023 by Hardie Grant Books,
an imprint of Hardie Grant Publishing

Hardie Grant Books (Melbourne)
Wurundjeri Country
Building 1, 658 Church Street
Richmond, Victoria 3121

Hardie Grant Books (London)
5th & 6th Floors
52–54 Southwark Street
London SE1 1UN

hardiegrant.com/books

Hardie Grant acknowledges the Traditional Owners of the Country on which we work, the Wurundjeri People of the Kulin Nation and the Gadigal People of the Eora Nation, and recognises their continuing connection to the land, waters and culture. We pay our respects to their Elders past and present.

NATIONAL LIBRARY OF AUSTRALIA

A catalogue record for this book is available from the National Library of Australia

Pasta et Al
ISBN 978 1 74379 900 0

10 9 8 7 6 5 4 3 2 1

Publisher: Michael Harry
Managing Editor: Penelope White
Project Editor: Antonietta Melideo
Editor: Andrea O'Connor
Design Manager: Kristin Thomas
Designer & Illustrations: Evi-O.Studio | Evi O, Susan Le & Kait Polkinghorne
Production Manager: Todd Rechner

Colour reproduction by Splitting Image Colour Studio
Printed in China by Leo Paper Products LTD.

FSC www.fsc.org MIX Paper from responsible sources FSC® C020056

The paper this book is printed on is from FSC®-certified forests and other sources. FSC® promotes environmentally responsible, socially beneficial and economically viable management of the world's forests.

About the Author

Alec Morris and his young sons, Aldo and Elio, are a team of playful pasta-makers determined to bring their favourite Sunday meal to your table.

Learning from his nonna at a very early age, Alec has been making pasta for over 30 years. His blog, *Pasta et Al*, began simply as a record of this weekly tradition as he passed it on to his children. However, it quickly grew into an international community drawn together by the trio's unique blend of old and new, heartfelt storytelling and, of course, tiny, squishy hands. They continue to inspire new pasta-makers, reinvigorate old ones and even gain the occasional endorsement from someone's nonna.

Alec has degrees in languages, international relations, history, and photography, and has called Canberra home for the past 15 years. Since commencing this book, he has returned west to Perth, where he now lives with his wife Rachel and their two sons.